growing your business

teach yourself®

growing your business

kevin duncan

For over 60 years, more than 50 million people have learnt over 750 subjects the **teach yourself** way, with impressive results.

be where you want to be
with **teach yourself**

For UK order enquiries: please contact Bookpoint Ltd, 130 Milton Park, Abingdon, Oxon OX14 4SB. Telephone: +44 (0) 1235 827720. Fax: +44 (0) 1235 400454. Lines are open 09.00–17.00, Monday to Saturday, with a 24-hour message answering service. Details about our titles and how to order are available at www.teachyourself.co.uk

Long renowned as the authoritative source for self-guided learning – with more than 50 million copies sold worldwide – the **teach yourself** series includes over 500 titles in the fields of languages, crafts, hobbies, business, computing and education.

British Library Cataloguing in Publication Data: a catalogue record for this title is available from the British Library.

First published in UK 2006 by Hodder Education, 338 Euston Road, London, NW1 3BH.

Typeset by Transet Limited, Coventry, England.
Printed in Great Britain for Hodder Education, a division of Hodder Headline, 338 Euston Road, London NW1 3BH, by Cox & Wyman Ltd, Reading, Berkshire.

Hodder Headline's policy is to use papers that are natural, renewable and recyclable products and made from wood grown in sustainable forests. The logging and manufacturing processes are expected to conform to the environmental regulations of the country of origin.

Impression number 10 9 8 7 6 5 4 3 2
Year 2011 2010 2009 2008 2007 2006

contents

dedication

My work is always dedicated to the special people in my life: my father James Grant Duncan, 1923–1989; my mother Anne; my extraordinary daughters Rosanna and Shaunagh; my brothers Robin and Alan; and my partner Sarah Taylor. People like this make the whole thing worthwhile.

acknowledgements

There are certain friends who are a constant source of inspiration when it comes to discussing business. We all agree that it's 1 per cent method, and 99 per cent about the people. So I salute the following true characters – thank you for your inspirational support: Cathy Johnson, Dave Hart, John Hamilton-Hunt, Melanie Ryder, Niclas Ljungberg, Nick Middleton, Paul Speers, Rassami Hök Ljungberg, Sara Tye and Simon Docherty.

And a very special mention to Sarah Taylor, who has endured me writing this book, and who has had almost all of it test-driven on her. The Sleeping Lion is ready to wake.

To those who have said amusing and inspirational things over the years, many of which are included here: Adam Morgan, Gary Miller-Cheevers, Martin Brooks, Micky Finn, Nick Hough.

And all those who contributed to the survey: Adam Sunderland, Ailsa Williams, Alex Aiken, Andrew White, Anthony Price, Belinda Lawson, Carol Dukes, Chris Hirst, Chris Matthews, Claire Walker, Daf Jones, David Bennett, Damian Clarkson, Denise Haire, Dominic Armstrong, Gary Miller-Cheevers, Gerry Hopkinson, Giles Fraser, Giles Gibbons, Gordon Haxton, Greg Mills, Gus Williams, Helen Ascott, Helen Edwards, Ian Fairbrother, Ian Farrow, Irma Hamilton-Hunt, Jamie Lister, Jim Marshall, John Owrid, Jonathan Harman, Julian Davies, Karen Brooks, Katrine Birk, Kirsten English, Lauren Richards, Laurence Green, Louise Wall, Marcel Feigel, Mark Joy, Mark Turner, Martin Deboo, Martin Roberts, Melanie Ryder, Neil Duffy, Nick Middleton, Nick Mustoe, Niclas Ljungberg, Nik Done, Paul

Ephremsen, Paul Simons, Paul Speers, Peter Gaze, Phil Georgiadis, Renée Botham, Richard Hytner, Robert Ashton, Robert Ray, Shaun Orpen, Stephen Martin, Steve Greensted, Stuart Rock, Sue Buckle, Tim Lawler, Tom Holmes, Tony Walford and Vanella Jackson.

about the author

Kevin Duncan worked in advertising and direct marketing for 20 years. For the last six years he has worked on his own as a business adviser, marketing expert and author. He teaches at Canterbury University, and advises various businesses in design, public relations, advertising, field marketing and accountancy, helping them with business strategy, marketing and training.

He has two daughters, Rosanna and Shaunagh, and lives in Westminster. In his spare time he travels to strange parts of the world, collects classic guitars and flies birds of prey.

His other book *Teach Yourself Running your own Business* is available through Hodder. He can be contacted at:

kevinduncan@expertadvice.co.uk

or you can look at his website:

expertadviceonline.com

1 introduction

Lots of people launch businesses. Not all know what to do next

In the last few years, I have spoken to over 1,000 people who have run their own businesses in one form or another. Much of their experience was used to develop the ideas in my previous book, *Teach Yourself Running your own Business*, and their reaction to that collected advice was most interesting. One particular question kept cropping up: what do you do *after* you've set up your own business? This is a truly fascinating area. One's first reaction is to assume that, just because someone has set up their own business, they should certainly know what to do with it thereafter. Indeed, you might even think that they would have worked that bit out *before* they started up. But life isn't like that. Lots of people establish their own business because they want to prove a point (to themselves or to their previous employers), because they are convinced there is a better way, or because they have an excellent idea that appears to have a potential market. They are entrepreneurial people. They are good at getting things underway, but they don't always think much further than that. They have fantastic energy and determination. And they can become bored fairly easily. So after the initial rush of enthusiasm that comes with getting everything underway, things settle into a rhythm that seems dull by comparison. This book looks at that next stage. It may well be growth. It may not. That depends on what you want from the business, and what you wish for yourself.

You cannot be prescriptive about growth

It is easier to be prescriptive about running a business than it is about growing or developing it. New businesses require a shape, and certain decisions to create that shape. But developing the business has to cope with an existing shape, or rip it up to engineer a new one. So this book avoids telling you precisely what to do, and instead offers new ways of thinking that should enable you to decide the future of your business for yourself. It's very much a case of 'try this, it might work.' It will certainly help any sole trader who is looking for inspiration to change the pattern of their work. But it will also help those who run larger 'small' businesses (with, say, up to 500 staff). The old adage that it is lonely at the top is confirmed whenever you ask the opinions of Managing Directors and Chief Executives in any sector. They almost always lack like-minded people with whom they can discuss the next round of challenges and, even if they do have such characters around, there is a strong chance that they are too close to the subject matter to apply any truly fresh thinking. As soon as these people have 'turned native', they cannot be objective about what needs to be done next. They have too much of a vested interest. So in those situations what is needed are new and different ways of thinking that can help push the business on to its next phase.

Introducing The CHEW system

The CHEW system is a gritty way of addressing the current state of your business, combined with a thoughtful and rigorous method for working out what to do next. The CHEW acronym is intended to work on various levels. It stands for Confront, Hone, Evolve, What next?

The Confront element forces those running businesses to tackle head-on the stage they have reached, with no fudging of the facts. It emphasizes the value of proper thought, and poses the rather tricky question: are you disciplined enough to be free?

The Hone phase whittles this information into manageable chunks by introducing three types of evolutive thinking – the facts, your own thoughts, and the wisdom of others. Stage one of this process reveals rivers and dams in your business (things that flow well and blockages that obstruct success). Stage two tells you how to heed your own counsel. And the wisdom of others is a fascinating survey of over 60 real people who pass on their experience of running businesses of various sizes by answering six critical questions that have a direct bearing on how to develop your business.

The Evolve part shows you how to distil, articulate and write down what you want for your business and, critically, for yourself. This involves setting up business tripwires that force the right things to happen, and the writing of your own Lifesmile Statement.

The What next? section takes a more whimsical look at the vagaries of business life – how far too many people confuse movement with progress, the fact that corporations don't have memories, and that everything may or may not be related to everything else. If that all sounds a bit ethereal, don't worry. As any good businessperson will tell you, it's the soft stuff that matters most, and this is simply an opportunity to confirm that the author knows he cannot organize the world in a uniform way.

Introducing evolutive thinking

Do you want to grow your business? Or develop it? Or evolve it? There is no set way to do it. Some believe a lot of it is down to luck, others swear by rigorous planning. Some suffer from post-launch blues, some from a three-year itch. Sometimes there is no itch. Whatever they call it, people who run businesses are always, one way or another, working on the 'next big thing'. Some desire expansion, others fear it because of the effect it may have on them, their staff, or their families. So, to strike an appropriate balance between prolific world domination at one end of the spectrum and total stasis at the other, I propose evolutive thinking. This does not presuppose that you wish for either extreme – simply that some form of forward motion on your terms is probably a desirable thing. That's why it is perfectly possible that the 'next big thing', might actually be very small. And why I have solicited the opinions of all sorts of business people for the breadth of their knowledge. No one is right or wrong, but they are, without exception, interesting.

The survey

The survey asked those running businesses of all types six tricky questions.

1. What is the hardest thing about growing your business?
2. Is growth always a good thing?
3. Did you ever suffer from post-launch blues or a three-year itch?
4. How do you plan the 'next big thing'?
5. If you could have known one thing when you started that you know now, what would it be?
6. Is there anything else you would like to pass on about growing or evolving your business?

As well as adding my own interpretation of the responses, the answers are grouped by company size to enable you to go straight to the views of those who run businesses of your size, or a size to which you aspire. They are divided into:

- Sole traders
- Small partnerships (two or three people)
- Fewer than 10 staff
- 10–50 staff
- More than 50 staff.

Summary: who is the book aimed at?

You should read this book if:

- You have launched your own business, run it for a while and are thinking: what now?
- You don't necessarily believe that relentless growth is always the answer
- You like the idea of a more reflective, non-macho approach to developing businesses
- You are a bit bored with your own ways of evolving your business and fancy a fresh perspective
- You are having a bit of trouble planning the 'next big thing'
- You want to read what 60 or more other people have to say in answer to the survey questions
- You are a good mate of the author and want to further his burgeoning writing career.

Kevin Duncan, Westminster, 2006

5 the CHEW system: what is it?

The CHEW system – what's it all about? Well, it is a gritty way of addressing the current state of your business, combined with a thoughtful and rigorous method for working out what to do next. The CHEW acronym is intended to work on various levels. It stands for Confront, Hone, Evolve and What next? Each section will explain in detail how it all works. Some people regard acronyms as a bit cheesy and trite, others find them very helpful in enabling them to remember all the stages of a process. Bosses often like them because they are good vehicles for helping their staff remember the plan or the vision. Either way, it's only four letters so it's not overly complicated, and it should help you to memorize the steps. Acronym fan or not, the word chew is chosen for a good reason – several in fact. Let's start by looking at what the word means.

Chew (verb): to masticate

That's straightforward enough, but it's when you add another word or two to this most interesting verb that things start to get interesting. When issues are complicated, we chew them over. When we are discussing things with others, we chew the fat, or the cud. When we damage something, we chew it up. The state of being chewed up means being nervous or worried about something. When the Americans reprimand someone, they chew them out. And sticky problems are often described as being chewy. So one way or another, there's quite a lot of chewing going on, and a lot of it is to do with business growing pains. So the central reason for choosing the word chew is that this book is all about contemplating how to grow your business, and that will certainly involve a lot of chewing things over. Or to put it another way: mental mastication. We will investigate all sorts of techniques for this in chapters 4 to 6. There is also a strong link here to the art of rumination.

Ruminate (verb): (of ruminants) to chew (the cud); (of people) to meditate or ponder upon

Ruminants are animals with stomachs that have four compartments. They chew all day to extract the necessary nutrients from the rather paltry grass they eat. If you think about it, it is remarkable that grass can create and sustain a cow or a camel, and yet it does. So they spend all day chewing the cud, or ruminating. When people ruminate, they ponder on something. If they become thoroughly lost in thought, they may even verge on meditation. It is a wonderful thing to do, and I commend it to you highly, as you will see in particular in chapter 3. The word ruminant can also be an adjective, so if a person is ruminant, then they are contemplating something.

Ruminant (noun): mammals with stomachs that have four compartments
Ruminant (adjective): meditating or contemplating in a slow quiet way

So the spirit of the CHEW system is to encourage you to think carefully about your business, what the true state of affairs is, and what exactly you are going to do to make the next move. This may be growth, or it may not, but we will come to all that later. The system has a shape and a method to it in order to help you organize your thinking. Random thoughts are sometimes quite brilliant, but they are by definition random. They may or may not occur when you want them. They may or may not be concerned with the bits of your business that really matter at that particular time. So the system is designed not to stifle your imagination, but to order your thoughts so as to increase the likelihood of you reaching a conclusion that helps you and your business on to the next helpful thing.

Confront

The first phase is called Confront. It is designed to force you to tackle head-on the stage your business has reached, with no fudging of the facts. It emphasizes the value of proper, clinical thought, and poses some rather tricky questions. So you have set up your business? So what? So you're in charge? So what? Are you disciplined enough to be free? What's the point? What's it all for? These are essentially the nasty questions that can keep a person awake at night, and they need serious thought to ensure your sustained happiness. The Confront phase also points out that thinking is free, so why don't we do more of it? The old adage 'I haven't had time to stop and think' afflicts pretty much everyone in modern business, so we owe it to ourselves to create the right conditions for a good old think from time to time.

Hone

The Hone phase whittles this information into manageable chunks by introducing three types of evolutive thinking. You might not think that the word evolutive exists, but it does. It's right there, in the dictionary.

> **Evolutive** (adjective): relating to, tending to, or promoting evolution

Note that the definition suggests that you relate, tend to, or promote evolution. These are all excellent nurturing words that can be applied to business thought. Chapters 4 to 6 will explore this in detail. The word evolution is carefully chosen because you may or may not want to grow your business relentlessly, but you will certainly want to evolve it. Human nature dictates that doing the same thing on the same scale in the same way for years becomes boring. So we crave evolution, whatever form it may take. There are three types of evolutive thinking proposed: the facts, your own thoughts, and the wisdom of others. Stage one of this process forces you to highlight rivers and dams in your business (things that flow well and blockages that obstruct success). Stage two tells you how to heed your own counsel. This is an important reminder to us all because we all know that decorators tend to have unpainted houses and doctors are quite capable of advising their clients not to smoke when in fact they do it themselves. So heeding your own counsel is important. The third stage is based mainly on the wisdom of others. This is a fascinating survey of over 60 people who have kindly passed on their experiences of running businesses of various shapes and sizes by answering six critical questions that have a direct bearing on business evolution. Put that lot together and you have a veritable powerhouse of evolutive thinking on which to base your next move.

Evolve

The Evolve phase is shorter because you have broken the back of it by now and done the majority of the hard work. It shows you how to distil, articulate and write down what you want for your business and, critically, for yourself. If you do the one without the other, you have only done half the job. In other words, there is no point in 'fixing' the business if you haven't taken the time to think about yourself. The business element involves setting up tripwires that force the right things to happen, whether you find it easy or not. That means less hassle, and less stress, over the coming year. The personal bit involves the writing of your own Lifesmile Statement. This has elements of lifestyle built into it, naturally, but the most important part is working out what really makes you happy. You will be forced to think about it, write it down and, once you have taken the trouble to do that, it tends to happen.

What next?

By the What next? section, we are nearly home and dry. It takes a more whimsical look at the vagaries of business life, in a discursive sort of way that reminds you that all business people face the same issues. It covers how far too many people confuse movement with progress, spending far too much time on activity rather than action. We will be emphasizing the value of outcome, not output. The point that corporations don't have memories is given a thorough working over in chapter 10, and we finish with a look at the notion that everything may or may not be related to everything else. If that all sounds a bit ethereal, don't worry. As any good businessperson will tell you, it's the soft stuff that matters most, and this is simply an opportunity to confirm that the world cannot be organized in a uniform way, so you had better get used to the idea.

Phase I: Confront

1 So you have launched your business. What now?
2 Are you disciplined enough to be free?
3 Thinking is free

Phase II: Hone

1 Evolutive thinking stage 1: Facts
2 Evolutive thinking stage 2: Own opinion
3 Evolutive thinking stage 3: Other people's wisdom

Phase III: Evolve

1 Set up your business tripwires and grenades
2 Write your own Lifesmile Statement

Phase IV: What Next?

1 Don't confuse movement with progress
2 Corporations don't have memories
3 Everything may or may not be related to everything else

figure 1 the CHEW system

phase I confront

In this phase you will learn:

- how to confront the issues in your business
- what to do after your business is successfully launched
- how to liberate yourself through discipline
- the art of proper thinking

So let's kick off with Phase I. It is called Confront. The dictionary definition of confront is to face boldly, or to bring together for comparison, and that is precisely what you need to do with yourself and your business in order to work out what needs to be addressed.

Confront (verb): to face boldly; to bring together for comparison

We start by asking some awkward questions, and then develop the idea of doing some hard thinking about what you have discovered.

- The first question (chapter 1) is: So you've launched your business. What now? Here we will question everything and force you to revisit all the issues that you probably thought about when you started, but may not have done since.
- Then we'll go on to ask in chapter 2: Are you disciplined enough to be free? Rather enigmatic perhaps, but there is a solid truth lurking beneath it. It takes careful thought and adherence to strong principles to have the business running as you want it, and on your terms. This level of integrity and solidity often drifts over time, and needs reasserting regularly.
- In chapter 3 we look at the whole area of thought. Thinking is free. How often do you do it? Every person running a business needs time to think, but frequently fails to create it often enough. So we will look at ways of helping that along.

That's the shape of Phase I. Right, so let's get cracking then.

01 so you have launched your business. what now?

In this chapter you will learn:

- **what to do after your business is successfully launched**
- **how to struggle with the issue of *what now?***
- **that you cannot be prescriptive about growth**
- **how to apply some tough thinking**
- **how to pose some nasty questions such as *so what?***

Lots of people launch businesses. Not all know what to do next

It's a tricky business. What exactly *do* you do after you've set up your own business? Or after you have been placed in charge of one and put in place all the things needed to fix the problems you were hired to solve. You have proved a point, and shown everybody (including yourself probably) that you can do it. Now what? Let's assume that the initial rush of enthusiam that comes with getting everything underway has settled down a bit, and that you are now restless again. It is time to look at the next stage. It might be growth. It might not. That depends on what you want for the business, and what you wish for yourself. One thing is for sure – it is not easy to plan down to the last detail, but you can certainly do some helpful thinking.

You cannot be prescriptive about growth

Growth is always an adventure, and it needs to be viewed as such, and approached with the right attitude.

> **'An adventure is an inconvenience rightly considered.'**
>
> *G. K. Chesterton*

Rushing into the unknown is all part of the thrill of running a business. It is all a bit of an adventure. Some people love it. Some crave it. Some find themselves in charge of businesses but didn't necessarily ask to be there. Businesses always have issues and problems. You can't have customers without having to sort out a lot of tricky stuff. You can't have staff without having to maintain them. So let's assume that you are in charge of a business. It doesn't matter whether you set it up yourself, or whether someone else did. The point is, it has been up and running for a while, and the launch phase is complete. The business is established. So what are you going to do now?

You've heard of tough love, well now's the time for some tough thinking

You'll have heard of tough love, when people need to be told the truth for their own good. Well now's the time for some tough thinking. That means more confrontation. Not with other people, but with the conflicting thoughts in your head. This tough thinking may apply to you personally, or to your business, and this book contains ways to approach both areas, because they are always interlinked. It is time to confront your demons. This is the basic dilemma all businesses face when they have set up, and have then paused to reflect, or have become restless. Let's start with a series of nasty questions that require candid answers. If you think you are not going to like some of the answers, then take some quiet time out and don't attempt the process when you are at work. And please, don't lie to yourself – it renders the whole exercise pointless and you are a grown-up now! Okay, take a deep breath.

Some nasty questions

- Are you happy?
- Are you in charge of your own destiny?
- Are you king of nothing?
- Are you proud of what you have achieved?
- Are you impressed with yourself?
- Are you status conscious?
- Are you out of your depth?
- Where does it all end?
- When does it all end?

What sort of answers have you come up with? This is not a psychological test, so there are no right and wrong ones, but what is the general shape? If you are essentially happy, and in charge of your own destiny, then you might as well stop reading this and go out for a celebratory meal immediately. If you conclude that you are king of nothing, then there is something wrong. If you find yourself in a top role purely for status reasons, or if you feel out of your depth, then we certainly have some work to do. If you have no idea when or where the whole thing is going to end, don't panic. That might not be the end of the world, but it is preferable if you can answer one or the other of them. If you can picture where it is all going to end, but not when, that's a good start because you know what you want but aren't too concerned about the immediate time frame. If you can envisage when you are going to conclude this thing, but not necessarily where, that could be okay. If you are not sure of either, some thought is required.

In my previous book, I extolled the virtues of asking yourself simple questions and being brutally honest about the answers. Questions such as: *why?* Now is the time to introduce another: *so what?* Although potentially annoying if addressed to someone else, it is a great leveller when you ask it of yourself. Try some of these for size.

Some So what? questions

- You're in charge. So what?
- You have lots of people reporting to you. So what?
- You have a large office. So what?
- You have your name on the door. So what?
- You are your own boss. So what?
- You earn more money than before. So what?
- Your sales are up this year. So what?
- Your profit is up on last year. So what?

You get the idea. There is no right or wrong answer, but hopefully you have stirred yourself up a bit. The knack is not to give any particular answer, but to know *why* you have given that answer. If you do know why, and are happy with that response, then excellent. If you are not happy with any particular answer, then you have some thinking to do on that topic. Once you get the hang of it, you can invent your own questions, so long as they are all personal to you, and so long as all the responses that you give are honest. Do not fall into the trap of self-delusion.

Can't get no satisfaction

Most people who run businesses are never quite satisfied, because they always feel they have unfinished business, no matter how well things are going. There's always something else that can be done. They are constantly dealing with an unfinished article. They may also be dealing with post-launch blues, or going through a three-year itch. 'Three-year itch' is of course a catch-all phrase for any kind of period of dissatisfaction, and the timing of it varies hugely, as we will see in chapter 6 (Other people's wisdom). For some it is three months, for some seven years, and for some it never comes at all. But if it does, it can eat away as insidious self-doubt, and it needs to be confronted urgently before it starts to ruin everything – that is the business *and* your sanity.

> **'Self-pity is the enemy of generosity.'** *Alexander Chancellor*

So what happens if you discover that, on reflection, you are not that happy with your state of affairs? Well, you have got some work to do. There is no room for self-pity here. Your friends and family won't enjoy it, nor will your staff if you have them and, ultimately, it is of no use to you either. So you need to understand *why* you are not happy, and set about trying to fix it.

> **'Do not weep; do not wax indignant. Understand.'**
>
> *Baruch Spinoza*

The key to this is *understanding*. There is no point sitting around bewailing the fact that things are as they are, when you could be spending time working out *why* they are as they are. Therein lies the potential to change things. Get to the heart of the matter, and concentrate on which bits you can influence personally, and who can help you attend to the rest. It is the solution you are after, not the waffle and preamble that takes you longer to get there. So spot the endgame, and head for that point straightaway.

> **'Almost every man wastes part of his life in attempts to display qualities that he does not possess.'**
>
> *Samuel Johnson*

Part of the reason may be that you are trying to do things that you do not enjoy, or that you are not particularly good at. There is no disgrace in not being brilliant at everything. In fact, there is barely anyone alive who is. So don't beat yourself up about it. Instead work out ways to circumnavigate areas that don't suit you, re-engineer the business so that you don't have to do them, or get other people in to do them for you. That might be staff, or one-off experts. Have a look at chapters 4 to 6 for effective ways to tackle this area.

'Even in slight things, the experience of the new is rarely without some stirring of foreboding.' *Eric Hoffer*

A lot of people do not like change. Indeed, they are often scared of it. There is nothing wrong with that feeling. So long as you don't allow it to be so overwhelming that it genuinely prevents you from any sort of forward motion. If you run your own business, you should be keen to move ever onward. If you run someone else's, equally you will not want to be doing the same thing all the time, so plunge in to the new with a sense of adventure. You might surprise yourself.

Chapter 1 recap

1. Are you being too prescriptive about growth?
2. Have you decided what to do next?
3. Do you regard the next step as an adventure?
4. Have you asked yourself the tricky questions?
5. Have you confronted the answers you didn't like?
6. Have you thoroughly understood why things are as they are?
7. Do you know what you are going to do to make things better?
8. Have you eliminated any self-pity?
9. Have you found solutions to cover for qualities you do not have?
10. Have you braced yourself for some tough thinking?

Success Story: Amy Watson, the IT supplier who got it just right

Greed and 'world domination' expansion plans can be the death of many a business. Amy knew this, and made sure that her growth plans were based on sound judgement rather than hubris. She had stood in bars with enough boastful businessmen to realize that talking big is only half the story. The phrase 'turnover is vanity, profit is sanity' was one of her favourites.

Amy ran an Information Technology training business, teaching people how to use all the new software packages that came onto the market. Developments were so rapid that there was always a good pipeline of people who needed to update their skills in this area. This forward motion was always tempered, however, by the natural inertia of human nature, and the fact that training is usually one of the first things to be cut or frozen when times get hard.

Amy did her launch research brilliantly, highlighting two top markets for her services: the financial industry for accounting-based software, and the creative industries for artistic, graphics-based software. She trained herself on the whole lot first and marketed herself to the relevant companies. After a year, when her personal time was almost fully booked, she recruited an expert in each category on a freelance basis to help. They were delighted to have the work and she did not want them on a payroll.

After three years, she had a pool of ten such freelancers, the knack being that they were only paid if she was. She then had enough in the bank to hire a low-cost room in which to hold the training. This was part of her plan to increase attendance and command a more premium price. The first of these was deliberately situated near to the city to attract the financial market.

After five years she was 85 per cent booked all year round, with two training centres and a pool of fifty trainers. The business was essentially self-sustaining, gave her a surplus of £10,000 a month, and enabled her to work a very pleasant ten-month year. Amy got there in judicious steps, and she never bragged once.

02 are you disciplined enough to be free?

In this chapter you will learn:

- **how to take a new look at your business**
- **if your new company is the same as the old company**
- **how to rip up the straitjackets you built yourself**
- **that efficiency is a sophisticated form of laziness**
- **if you are suffering from attitude sickness**

I once met an accountant in Kent. He was a very thoughtful guy, clearly intelligent, and seemingly successful. He had left a larger accountancy practice to set up his own because he felt there was definitely a better way. Excellent. This is the sort of flair and determination that keeps business vital. I then test-drove on him one of my theories about how people approach the administrative aspects of their new businesses, and asked: 'How did you design the administrative systems in your new venture?' The answer held little surprise. 'Oh,' he said, 'we based them on the ones from my previous place.'

This anecdote is not designed to humiliate the man in question, but simply to illustrate one of the oldest pitfalls in the book. That is to say, many people who strike out for a brave new dawn simply end up generating their own version of what they had before, complete with all its flaws and drawbacks. It isn't always the case, but it often is.

New company: same as the old company?

For those of you who like a bit of rock music, you will be familiar with the line in the Who song *Won't get fooled again: 'Meet the new boss. Same as the old boss.'* You would do well to ask yourself whether this has inadvertently become the case with you personally, or the company you now run. On reflection are you simply replicating the past? Have you invented a genuinely new mousetrap, or is it unnervingly similar to the old one? So here they come again – more nasty questions.

> **'The truth will set you free, but first it will piss you off.'**
>
> *Gloria Steinem*

- Is your company unnervingly similar to the one you left because you were supposedly fed up with it?
- Have you started behaving similarly to your old boss?
- Did you rather lazily imitate the processes and systems at your previous company when designing your current ones?
- Do you have a nagging suspicion that certain things around here do not work particularly well?

- Do you suspect that there is a better way of doing these things?
- Can you think of what they might be?

If the answer to any of these questions is yes, then we have some work to do. It's all about instilling the discipline, both mental and structural, that will free you up to do the rewarding bits more easily and frequently. That's what the question (Are you disciplined enough to be free?) is all about. It means getting rid of any straitjackets that are preventing you or your business from having a decent time of it and being a reasonable success. These straitjackets might be mental, they might be physical, or they might be process-based. Let's have a look at the different types.

Ripping up the straitjackets you built yourself

What's all this about then? Surely, I hear you cry, I haven't built any straitjackets for myself? Well you won't have done it intentionally, but you may have done it nevertheless. What we are referring to here is something that severely limits or restricts you personally, or an aspect of your business. When you think about it, there may be more of them than you would initially like to admit.

Straitjacket (noun): a severe limitation or restriction

Grab a pen and paper, and write these three headings on it, leaving space in the middle to fill out your answers.

1 Mental straitjackets
2 Physical straitjackets
3 Process straitjackets

Have a look at each, and write down your instinctive reaction to what these might be. If none occur, this could be very good news in that you may well be a highly liberated person, free of constraints, running a business that is brilliantly designed and operates perfectly. How many people do you know in that position? More likely, you have reservations and concerns about all sorts of issues. If the page is blank, or you have already finished with your initial thoughts, then try these prompts.

Mental straitjackets

- Do I have time to generate new ideas?
- Am I *capable* of originating new ideas?
- If not, do I know anyone who is that can help?
- Am I able to implement all the ideas I want?

Physical straitjackets

- Is my working environment appropriate?
- Do I have the right blend of staff or colleagues?
- Do I spend too much time travelling?
- Am I frequently in the wrong place to get things done?

Process straitjackets

- Do I spend too much time in meetings?
- Do our systems work well?
- Do things get bogged down unnecessarily too often?
- Did I design these systems myself, or were they borrowed from somewhere else?
- Do they genuinely represent the right tools for the job?

If the answers to these questions do not fill you with glee, then chances are it is time to rip up some straitjackets. If that fills you with dread, it shouldn't. Change is good. Trust your instincts. If you know in your heart that something doesn't work very well, and you have now had the courage to confess it unwittingly on paper by answering the questions honestly, then it is time for action. Reassure yourself with the knowledge that, whatever it is, it *is* broken, and it *does* need fixing. Once you have taken a deep breath and fixed it, you will have far less hassle from that moment on. Of course, this part of the process only forces you to identify the trouble, not cure it. If you are an excellent problem solver, then you may immediately know how to design your own new mousetrap. If not, don't worry, we will work our way through plenty of methods in phases II and III.

'Reality is the leading cause of stress among those in touch with it.' *Lily Tomlin*

It takes guts to answer the nasty questions honestly. It takes discipline and determination to do something as a result to improve things. This is your job because you are in charge. Whether that is in charge of 100 people or just yourself doesn't make a jot of difference. It's still down to you. Scary? Perhaps, but it shouldn't be. You are either paid well to do precisely that, or you are doing something because of what you believe in. Either way, it's your job, and the main beneficiary will usually be you. If you take the tough medicine now, you will have a more pleasant time in the future.

We have all heard the maxim *Work to live or live to work?* Which applies to you? Do you work mindlessly because it's there? Or do you use your work as a means to a more fulfilling life? Assuming you would prefer the latter, you need to apply strong discipline to get the business working for you, not the other way round. Let's try another one: *Rule to work or work to rule?* Do you let the strictures of working practices constrain your ability to enjoy working life and flourish in it? Or do you master the situation and make it work for you? The choice is yours. If by any chance it is the former, then I am afraid you may have turned native.

Turning native

What does this mean? It means that you have lost the capability to think independently. It means that you sound and act just like everybody else. The old joke goes like this: when management consultants have been working with their clients for too long, if you look at a video of a meeting between them, with no prior knowledge of who is who, you will not be able to differentiate between the consultants and the clients. Why? Because they are all speaking the same language. Using the same jargon. Wearing the same clothes. The consultants have turned native and are losing their value to their customers. If this is happening to you and your colleagues, change it immediately.

> **'When two people in business always agree, one of them is unnecessary.'** *William Wrigley Junior*

It's true isn't it? Under-confident people fail to express their opinion whilst simultaneously failing to recognize that their opinion is precisely what they are paid for. This is true of everybody – staff and consultants. If you don't have a view, what are you there for? So, make sure that you are disciplined enough not to turn native, and that you stay true to your opinions.

> **'An optimist sees an opportunity in every calamity. A pessimist sees a calamity in every opportunity.'**
>
> *Winston Churchill*

So we have spent some time looking at the tethers and straitjackets that constrain your business. You should now be turning your mind to how you can liberate yourself and your business systems to get on and enjoy a better work–life balance. Churchill had a point. What do you see? Glass half empty? Or half full? Or, indeed, do you give a stuff about the supposed glass at all? And what's in the glass, by the way? Methylated spirits or champagne? Life is random, and it is almost impossible to plan. So there will be calamities of a type pretty much every day of the week. But that doesn't mean it's the end of the world, and it doesn't mean you can't generate something positive out of it. So it is your job to engineer an opportunity out of whatever circumstances confront you. That's what this phase is all about: confrontation. That means confronting yourself, and the realities of your business.

Growing panes: a new look through the business window

Here's a little exercise that might help disentangle the good and bad bits of your working life and your business practices. You've heard of SWOT analysis, and various systems of analysis such as the Boston Matrix. Well this is the world's simplest one. Take a piece of paper and draw a windowpane on it. On the vertical axis, write GOOD at the top, and BAD at the bottom. On the horizontal axis, write OLD on the left, and NEW on the right. Now take a little time to categorize your habits and techniques. If something you usually do is old and good, then it goes in the top left quadrant, and so on. You will quickly build up a picture of the proportion of good/bad/old/new approaches that you use. Now do the same for those of your business.

If you have several practices in the 'Good and Old' segment, then that is fine. They have obviously stood the test of time, and do the job.

If you have several of them in the 'Good and New' section, even better. This means you are generating new ideas that really work. A blend of old and new is healthy, because it suggests good thinking at the outset, followed by fresh ideas thereafter.

If there is anything in the 'New and Bad' area, it needs careful analysis. It takes guts to reject an idea or process that has only recently been introduced. But surgery here may well be necessary. There may be a case for concluding that the jury is still out so a decision should be given a little more time. But more likely than not, the bad item will remain bad no matter how long you leave it, and the sooner it goes the better. This type of decision can be unpopular, particularly if colleagues have a vested interest, but a bad, ineffective process or idea is just that, and it needs to be eliminated quickly.

Anything in the 'Old and Bad' quadrant is clearly a disaster and has to go immediately.

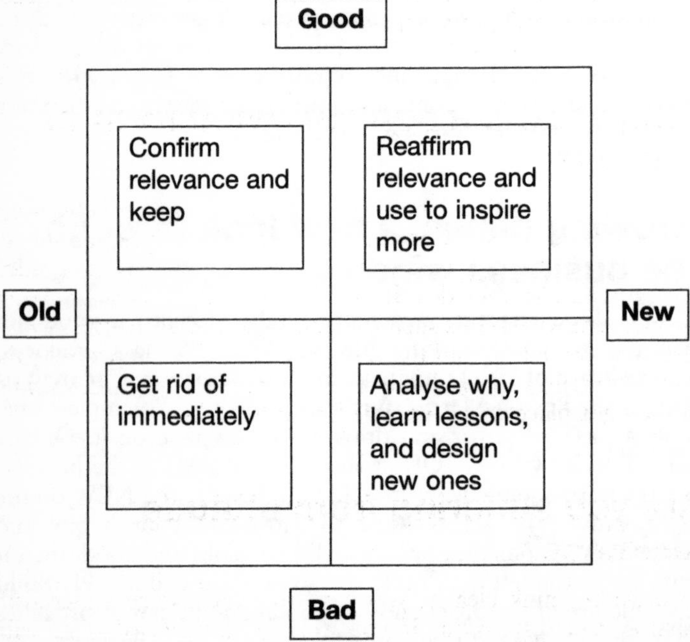

figure 2 the growing pane

'Planning is for the poor.' *Robert Evans*

I have put this quote in to spark a debate. Personally I think it is rubbish. Working out what you want to do and then sorting it out is one of the great fundamentals of having a decent life and a sane mind. You don't have to have endless spreadsheets or spend months over it. Just work out what you want to do, and then do it. The time you dedicate to thinking about things will serve you well when you have to get on and do whatever you have decided. But don't spend too long over it. Trust your instincts. You only have to do three things. It is a fairly straightforward business to write down, but somewhat harder to do. Here they are:

1 Get your head straight
2 Decide what you want to do
3 Do it

Phase I (Confront) is designed to help you sort out point 1. Phase II (Hone) attends to point 2. And Phase III (Evolve) covers point 3. So if you have trouble with any of the three points, head to the relevant chapters right now if you want.

Efficiency is a sophisticated form of laziness

This was an idea that I introduced in *Teach Yourself Running your own Business* (Chapter 8, page 99). Think about it carefully. The more sorted you are, the less you need to panic. We will pursue the idea further in chapter 7 (Set up your business tripwires). It is such a simple notion. Get the functional elements organized, and the rest slots into place. However, this level of organization will only be of limited use if your head isn't in the right place. Your attitude has to be right too.

Are you suffering from attitude sickness?

In order to think clearly, you have to have a decent blend of passion and dispassion. If you are horribly biased, you will make poor decisions. Rose-tinted spectacles are as useless as outright cynicism. (For a more detailed debate on cynicism and scepticism, have a look at chapter 5). You need a balance, otherwise you will become a danger to yourself. Sounds extreme? Not really. Poor thought leads to unsuccessful management and unsuccessful businesses, and you do not want that state of affairs on your hands. It is all about keeping the mystery alive. In the next chapter, we are going to develop some ways of doing this, but meanwhile, take a moment to reflect on the nasty questions in this chapter and chapter 1, and consider whether you have genuinely confronted the awkward stuff. Confront the tough issues and ask yourself: Am I disciplined enough to be free? Don't fudge the answer. If you do, you won't get anywhere, and you certainly won't be free.

> **'Anything can happen in life, especially nothing.'**
>
> *Michel Houellebecq*

Chapter 2 recap

1. Are your 'new' approaches the same as your old ones?
2. If so, what are you going to do about it?
3. Have you identified any mental, physical or process straitjackets?
4. If so, what are you going to do about it?
5. Have you turned native?
6. If so, what are you going to change, and how?
7. Have you filled out the Growing Panes grid?
8. Have you got rid of any bad things it revealed?
9. What have you done about being more organized?
10. Is your attitude right?

Cautionary Tale: Paul Dunn, the impatient Finance Director

Paul was a trained accountant who started in the finance department of a construction company and eventually became the Finance Director. He grew with the company, and after eight years it had become an established top three player in its market.

After enjoying the scale and status for a while, Paul became bored and hankered after doing his own thing. He decided to leave and set up a roving finance service, offering outsourced financial back-up services to companies who either had problems in that area, or who were too small to afford a Finance Director of their own.

The principle seemed reasonable enough - he would start with his construction contacts, and then branch out to advise companies in other markets, because he reckoned his skills were transferable. All fine so far, but when he started working on his own, he missed the status and the support services of his previous company. He simply didn't have the patience to build his business. Instead, he talked in generalities to potential customers, and was found wanting on the delivery. They wanted stuff done, and he was talking broad concepts. Or, to put it another way, they wanted the foundations built and he was describing the penthouse flat.

He probably would have been all right if he had paused at the outset to think carefully about the nature of work that he would pick up in the early days. A quick bit of thought here would have demonstrated that, in all likelihood, his early customers would be small fry. Could he live with that? Would he be happy to muck in until the cash in his new business enabled him to hire someone else to do the grunt work?

If he had been more honest with himself before setting up on his own, he might have realized that he just wasn't cut out for it. Paul was not a success on his own. He soon returned to a conventional Finance Director job in a medium-sized firm, surrounded by all the support services that made him feel good in the first place.

03 thinking is free

In this chapter you will learn:

- **that thinking is free, so do it more often**
- **why the next big thing might be small**
- **that a strategy is simply when you have decided what to do**
- **KISS: Keep It Simple and *Sensible***
- **KITSCH: Keep It Terribly Simple and Cool Headed**

Thinking is free, so do it more often

'I haven't had time to think.'

How many times have we heard that said? Millions of people say it every day in all walks of life, let alone in business. What does it actually mean? If you analyse the phrase carefully, it is complete nonsense. Every sentient being spends the entire day thinking, absorbing circumstances, and reacting to them. Of course, the phrase is not literal. What it really means is:

'I haven't had time to pause and think about the things that really matter, because lots of irrelevant stuff has got in the way.'

Aha. That's more accurate, and because businesses usually generate vast amounts of irrelevant stuff, businesspeople are very prone to the problem of not having enough thinking time. This is a tragedy, and it is your job to create the appropriate time to rectify the position. Why is this so important? Because, although you may claim that you are too busy to create the time, if you haven't worked out whether what you are doing is the *right* thing, then you may only be busy pursuing all the wrong things. In my previous book, *Teach Yourself Running your own Business,* I asserted that you should never do anything unless you know why you are doing it (page 91). This sounds blindingly obvious, and yet people frequently do.

So now is the time to get thinking. It is a free activity. All you have to do is set aside the time and create the appropriate conditions. Some people like total peace and seclusion, others like something to shake them up. Work out your style by answering these questions to help you develop different ways of creating thinking time.

Are you likely to have some decent ideas if you:

- Sit on top of a mountain
- Have a massage
- Get on the running machine
- Go for a jog
- Disappear to a country cottage
- Drink a bottle of quality wine
- Go for a bike ride
- Leave the country for the day
- Take a ride in a hot air balloon

- Visit the zoo
- Go fishing?

You get the idea. The activity or circumstance doesn't matter, so long as it is different from where you normally are, and what you normally do.

> **'A great many people think they are thinking, when they are merely rearranging their prejudices.'** *William James*

If everything is too samey, or things aren't going that well, it's time for a re-think. And that does not mean rearranging your prejudices, or dreaming up new reasons to prove that you are right about something. It means taking a hard look at what you've got and working out whether it is any good or not, and whether you like your circumstances. If you have any doubts about any aspect of your life or business, it has to be done. Even in the unlikely event that you don't have any concerns at all about anything, it is still a great thing to do. Everything can always be made better or more stimulating.

Try this. It might just work

You have to enter the thinking process in the right frame of mind. It's no use being petrified, depressed, cynical, paranoid, resentful, jaded, or any other negative emotion. It is okay to be a bit vexed or concerned. It is all right to be mildly sceptical. It is fine to be quizzical. In fact, that should be positively encouraged. Your objective should be to let a little light in on your circumstances and view it as though you were someone else looking at you. Strange, and quite detaching, but ultimately rewarding. Start with some general questions:

- Do you want evolution or revolution?
- Are you facing hard or soft decisions?
- Are you planning the 'next big thing'?

Be positive. You have to believe, 'If I try this, it might just work'.

Why the next big thing might be small

A lot of people get hung up on planning the 'next big thing'. But who is to say that the next big thing has to be big? Sometimes tiny increments of change make amazing things happen. If you are unconvinced of this, read Malcolm Gladwell's book, *The Tipping Point*. It demonstrates how little things can make a big difference, if cunningly applied. If you can't be bothered to buy the book or, rather more importantly, actually read the thing, then you will find a summary of it in the appendix. So don't panic about the fear that you need to come up with something outstandingly original. People rarely do. Occasionally someone like Edison will invent a light bulb, but that's a bit beyond our remit here. If by any chance you are a genius, then put this book down immediately – there's nothing I can teach you.

> **'God is in the details.'** *Anonymous artist*

There has been a huge amount of hoo-ha about 'the big idea'. Nothing wrong with that, but when you run a business, there is also great mileage to be had from lots of little ideas. Little ideas are great. They are less hard to come up with, they are usually cheaper and easier to implement, and they can be done more quickly. This enables you to work out rapidly whether they are any good or not. No one wants to admit that a big idea is rubbish once it has been implemented, so they are hard to rectify even if everybody can see that they aren't working very well. An example of this would be when Coca-Cola replaced their original version with a new one. Eventually they had to reissue it as Coke Classic. They got it right in the end, but it took a while for anyone to admit that the new 'big idea' wasn't working. In comparison, little ideas can be test-driven constantly, refined, enlarged, developed or withdrawn with the minimum of fuss. Try making your next big thing small. You might surprise yourself.

A strategy is when you have decided what to do

Complicated thinking is another cul-de-sac. Do not fall into the trap of thinking that an idea needs to be complicated, or that your route to it needs to be either. Good ideas are usually simple, as is the means by which they are conceived. Most people have heard of the KISS acronym, Keep It Simple Stupid. Whilst I admire the sentiment behind it, I am not a fan of the Stupid bit. You are not stupid, nor are most people who run businesses. So I have taken the double liberty of both adapting KISS, and inventing a new one: KITSCH. Here they are.

KISS: Keep It Simple and *Sensible*

It's the sensible bit that makes the difference for me. You're not daft, and you instinctively know what is likely to work. So keep it sensible as well as simple. This acronym may or may not be memorable because it has the same letters as the old one. So here is a new version that makes it clearer. It is longer and, of course, it presupposes that you can remember how to spell KITSCH, but it makes the point. In this one, the Sensible element is represented by the words Cool Headed, and the simplicity part is additionally emphasized by the adjective Terribly.

KITSCH: Keep It Terribly Simple and Cool Headed

The *Terribly* element here forces you to be ruthless about the simplicity of the idea. If you can't express it in one or two sentences, it is probably too complicated. If your mate who doesn't know your industry can understand it, it is probably all right. It doesn't mean it is any good, but at least it's clear. Then comes the cool headed part. There is no point in generating a head of steam about a new idea until you have worked it through properly. Passion is good. Enthusiasm is as well. But not if either are misdirected. If you let your heart run away with an idea before you have worked it out properly, you will waste your time and possibly your money.

> **'You do not really understand something unless you can explain it to your grandmother.'** *Albert Einstein*

This approach is simple, but not simplistic. It means you are not allowed to wrap yourself up in jargon. No complicated words! No spreadsheets! Just a pen and plenty of paper, your preferred thinking conditions, and an appropriate chunk of time dedicated to the matter in hand. If you need a little help and stimulation to increase the chances of your having some decent ideas, there are hundreds of books dedicated to the subject. One of the best is *Flicking your Creative Switch* by Wayne Lotherington. Once again, if you don't have the time to get hold of a copy, there is a synopsis for you in the appendix. Don't say I don't look after you.

Here are some other enigmatic thoughts to help you along:

- Stand back and take a closer look
- Death to compromise
- Look before you reap
- Other people's thoughts can't kill you, but your own could
- Other people's thoughts can't kill you, but your own could keep you alive
- Start with a bang, then bang again
- Watch for shapes, then nip into the gaps
- Ski off-piste for once
- When the others zig, zag. Then zog.

We will do lots more of this in Phase II. One thing is for sure: it takes time and concentration, so don't think you can get away with a quick fix or a cursory skim over the issues. Muster all your mental energy and create the right conditions to allow your thoughts to flow properly.

> **'If a problem is hard, think, think, then think again. It will hurt at first, but you'll get used to it.'** *Barbara Castle*

The business press has recently become riddled with comment on, and reference to, Thought Leadership, so if we are discussing the process of thinking, then we had better have a look and work out what on earth it is.

So what exactly is thought leadership?

I headed straight for the *Economist Guide to Management Ideas* (2003), but Thought Leadership wasn't in there. Strange. That either means that the idea is so new that it didn't exist in 2003, or that Thought Leadership isn't a management idea. Not believing either explanation, I reached for *Eating the Big Fish*, by Adam Morgan (1999). Aha, so it's not a new idea! This guy is something of a world expert on the matter. He describes Thought Leadership as 'the brand in the category that everyone talks about. While not the biggest, it is the brand that is getting the most attention. It's the one that is seen to be picking up momentum, entering the popular culture.' You've guessed it, the book is summarized for you in the appendix, because it is a really good rundown on how to make your business competitive when you do not have the resources of the big players in the market.

According to David Bolchover, writing in *The Times,* 'the term is used to describe ideas deemed to be innovative, supposedly allowing proactive "thought leaders" to move ahead of their competition, the slow-moving and reactive "thought followers".' He goes on to assert that 'genuinely new ideas in business are usually the preserve of start-up companies and entrepreneurs who have much to gain and little to lose'. There is much truth in that, although I doubt if those in charge of big companies would wish to admit it, and I doubt if those running small businesses would agree that they have little to lose. Judging by those I have spoken to, they feel they have everything to lose, but they are getting on with it anyway. He finishes by pointing out that 'those who claim the mantle of "thought leadership" are often simply following the follower of the thought leader. True thought leaders would never bother labelling themselves as such. They're too busy trying to make money.' Quite right. If you ever take the time to chat to someone who is an entrepreneur, you will find that they never describe themselves as one. *'Pleased to meet you, I'm an entrepreneur!'* I don't think so. It would be the same as describing your own trousers as cool. The moment you say it, it is no longer true.

So don't get hung up on trendy concepts like Thought Leadership. It is completely irrelevant to your central concern, which is to have a few good, simple, and quite possibly small, ideas that will contribute to the continuing success of your business, and your mental wellbeing.

'The mark of an educated mind is to be able to entertain an idea without accepting it.' *Aristotle*

You have now pretty much completed your preparation for quality thinking. Be open-minded about what you come up with. Remember the *Sensible* element of the revised KISS principle. Adopt the attitude that 'if I try this, it might just work'. Consider the small stuff as well as the large, and steer clear of supposed big ideas and management concepts that could distract you from the relevance of a clear, simple idea. That's the end of the Confront phase. In phase II (chapters 4 to 6) we are going to examine the three types of evolutive thinking.

Chapter 3 recap

1 Have you created the time to think?
2 If so, when exactly, and for how long?
3 Where are you going to do your thinking?
4 How is this environment different from your normal one?
5 Have you consulted any relevant books?
6 Have you examined and dismissed distracting management concepts?
7 Are you prepared to be open-minded?
8 Are you ready to consider small things as well as large?
9 How are you going to keep it simple?
10 Are you genuinely prepared to try out the ideas you generate?

Success Story: Mike Simmons, the market researcher who emulated the big boys from the beginning

Setting the right tone is always difficult when running a company. Sometimes it is called culture. Sometimes style. Whatever you call it, it all starts at the beginning, and it starts at the top.

Mike worked for a large market research company, and after a few years he concluded that the company's culture just wasn't his style. After a lot of thought, he did two things – he decided to leave, and he spent a long time working out what style of company he would like to set up.

This process was not borne out of arrogance. Mike knew in his heart that there is simply no point in working for a company if you don't really fit in with their way of doing things. So he wrote down the sort of company he would be proud of working for, and set about creating it. The business plan and, crucially, the recruitment policy, directly enacted his closely held beliefs.

Part of this belief was not to kowtow to larger firms. He couldn't stand it. He insisted that all his people could hold their own with the big boys. Again, this was not to manifest itself in arrogance, simply in the kind of intellectual quality and operational integrity that you would expect from the best in any field of business.

His staff loved it, because it imbued them with a much higher level of respect than they had experienced in their former jobs. His people were trusted and given a lot of rope. As a result, they behaved highly responsibly with clients, and enjoyed the sort of autonomy that suggests quality. That of course, meant they could charge more as a company, and all enjoy top salaries.

This happy state of affairs all stemmed from Mike's broadmindedness at the outset. He set the style, and success followed.

phase II hone

In this phase you will learn:

- **how to hone your thinking into manageable chunks**
- **the art of Foo fighting**
- **a new method of evolutive thinking**

Phase II of the CHEW system is called Hone. The definition of hone is to sharpen or polish something. In the old days this would have been done with a hone or whetstone, in order to give a smooth finish to a blade or artefact. Over time, though, the word has been applied to non-physical items such as thoughts and ideas. So when we hone something, we sharpen it and smarten it up in readiness for its intended use. So this phase is all about getting the ideas in shape so that they can serve a useful purpose. It takes a bit of sweat and some judicious application to determine how to generate decent thoughts, and how to judge whether or not they are any good. Any fool can have an idea, but the knack is to have the clarity and objectivity to admit if the idea has any merit, particularly if you thought of it yourself.

Hone (verb): to sharpen or polish with a hone or whetstone; to impart a smooth finish

We will start by introducing the basic idea of evolutive thinking, then we will work through the three types.

- Chapter 4 looks at the **Facts**, and forces you to consolidate them into manageable chunks to work out what to do next. There is no room here for opinion – just fact. We will look at rivers and dams. These are the bits in your business that flow well or cause blockages. After working that out, we draw from the world of ballistics to categorize the facts and apply some common sense analysis. If the process comes unstuck at any point, we will always come back to the vital question: remind me, what *was* the original idea?
- Chapter 5 examines your **Own** opinions. What do *you* think about your business, and what do *you* personally think should happen next? This is all about heeding your own counsel. We all have examples of people who give great advice but fail to pay attention to it themselves. This chapter highlights that point and encourages you to pay attention to your instincts more.
- Chapter 6 looks at the wisdom of **Others**. This is a substantial survey of over 60 business people from all sorts of sectors, and here we can learn from their experience and see what application it may have to the matter in hand.

Foo fighting

Those of you who like acronyms may have noticed that the three chapters form the acronym FOO: Facts, Own, Others. Some of you may have heard of the rock band Foo Fighters, but may not know whether that is an original name, or whether it was borrowed from somewhere. In fact, it is taken from the term given to UFOs by World War II pilots in the US Air Force. So in phase II we are going to do some Foo fighting of our own. We will deal with the facts first, then your own opinions, then those of others. Those are the three parts of the evolutive thinking technique and, by the end of it, we will have a veritable powerhouse of information with which to grow your business.

Why evolutive thinking?

We have already touched on the notion that relentless growth is not the be-all-and-end-all of business. It may be good, but sometimes it may not. There are some particularly vociferous opinions about this question in chapter 6, but for the moment let's just be open-minded about it. You may favour growth or you may not, but few would deny that some form of development is always desirable. This is because we all like forward motion and we all get bored. Hence the idea of evolution. Everything eventually evolves into something else. Most of us have spent time discussing the 'evolution versus revolution' debate in various business contexts. So let's examine what it all means and try to work out how you would like to evolve your business. Evolution is a gradual change in the characteristics of something. Now of course some people don't like gradual change because it isn't fast enough, but it rather depends on what timescale one is looking at. Gradual change can be good if it allows you to fine-tune things as you go along without making a hash of them. That's why we discussed why the next big thing might be small in so much detail.

Evolution (noun): a gradual change in the characteristics of something; a pattern formed by a series of movements

The other aspect of evolution is that it also refers to a pattern formed by a series of movements. In other words, your business has an historical shape that can be identified, examined, and in some cases used to predict what is coming next. So the word evolutive is simply the adjective that describes this sort of approach.

Evolutive (adjective): relating to, tending to, or promoting evolution

It is probably not a fluke that the verbs used to articulate the definition here are all nurturing words: relating, tending, and promoting. So we will be encouraging you to relate to your business, to tend to it, and to think about how to promote it.

Evolutive thinking is a method of thought that encourages you to relate to, tend to, and promote the evolution of your business. It is also helpful to define what it is not, by contrasting it with its opposite. You may or may not have come across the word involution. It either describes something that is involved or complicated, or that is reducing in size. We do not wish for either of these in relation to your business.

Involution (noun): the state of being involved or complicated; reduction in size

The adjective associated with involution is involute. It is sufficiently obscure to convince the American software on my computer that it is a spelling mistake, but it isn't. Have a look at an unabridged dictionary. It means complex, intricate or involved, and this is precisely the opposite of the type of thinking that we want to embark upon. So let's keep it simple and clear.

Involute (adjective): complex, intricate or involved

That's the shape of phase II. Now let's get on with some Foo fighting, and some evolutive thinking.

04 evolutive thinking stage 1: facts

In this chapter you will learn:

- **how to establish the true facts about your business**
- **how to identify rivers and dams in your business**
- **how to apply common sense analysis**
- **to admit if something was a fluke**
- **always to return to the original idea**

Stage 1 of the process is based solely on the facts. At this point we are not interested in your opinion, or those of others. This is not because they are not valid or useful, but because they place an angle on the facts that will hinder us at first. So we are going to get the truth out on the table and examine it. This is what a client of mine used to call 'having the drains up'. If you find yourself fudging the answers, rip them up and start again. We do not want our thinking to suffer from factual pollution.

Rivers and dams

First of all, imagine your business as a series of rivers and dams. These will be areas where everything is flowing well, or where there are frequently blockages that prevent you from conducting your business properly. Before you start, consider whether this process should be conducted on your own, or in the presence of others. If you are self-employed, or in charge of a company whose every workings are well known to you, then it might be a solo project. If not, it might be a suitable methodology for a brainstorm or awayday. The latter will be appropriate if you are unaware of all the facts yourself. After you have read how the process works, revisit this point because once you have seen all the questions you will have a clearer idea of whether you are fully qualified to answer them all or not. The first step is to ask some questions and write down the answers.

Remember rivers are things that flow well, and dams are places where they do not. We will start with the good stuff.

- Where are the rivers?
- How many of them are there?
- How large?
- How small?
- How many in total?

Put that to one side for a minute and take a deep breath. We are moving on to the not-so-good things.

- Where are the dams?
- How many of them are there?
- How large?
- How small?
- How many in total?

And put that list on the side. If it was a harrowing exercise, go for a walk or pour a stiff drink. Now answer the next question.

- Which do you have more of – rivers or dams?

This basic exercise should allow you to see at a glance what works in your business, and what doesn't. It will also reveal straightaway whether the business has more good things going on than bad, or vice versa. Don't panic at this stage if there seem to be way more dams than rivers. That's what we are here to sort out.

Send it down to the boys in forensic or go completely ballistic?

The next step is examining the truth. I used to work with a guy who, whenever we received a written request from a client, would say: 'Send it down to the boys in forensic'. The gist of it was that we needed the full rundown on the subject matter and the task in hand before we could start pontificating about any possible solutions. He was right. These days, they call it strategic planning. Whatever you call it, it needs to be a great inquisition of all the available information. To get to the heart of the matter, it is worth looking at the definitions of forensic and forensics.

Forensic (adjective): relating to, or used in, a court of law

Forensic as an adjective means relating to, or used in a court of law. That means whatever it refers to must be solely concerned with the facts. Strangely though, the noun forensics refers to the study of formal debating, which is an opinion-based and non-factual pursuit.

Forensics (noun): the art or study of formal debating

So we are going to deploy a different, more scientific term to define the stage of our factual line of enquiry. The inspiration comes from the world of ballistics. Ballistics is only concerned with the facts, and at this stage, so are we. We are going to concentrate on the structural elements of your business, the tangible ones. Using the language of ballistics, we will divide the business into manageable chunks that we can then analyse.

Ballistics (noun): the study of the flight dynamics of projectiles; the interaction of the forces of propulsion, projectile aerodynamics, atmospheric resistance and gravity

Get out another clean sheet of paper and split it into five sections, each with a heading: projectiles, propulsion forces, aerodynamics, resistance, and gravity. This is what the headings refer to:

- **Projectiles**: who, or what, is heading where?
- **Propulsion forces**: who, or what, is making them do that?
- **Aerodynamics**: who, or what, has good momentum behind it?
- **Resistance**: who, or what, is resisting forward motion?
- **Gravity**: is there anything structural that anchors any of this?

Don't fill the headings in at this stage. Put the piece of paper to one side. You might need it in a minute.

'Men occasionally stumble over the truth, but most of them pick themselves up and hurry off as if nothing happened.'

Winston Churchill

Common sense analysis

Now it is time to analyse what you've got. Stick to the facts and nothing else at this stage. We want the truth and nothing but. Don't ignore it. If you do, it will still be there tomorrow. Use your common sense. Common Sense Analysis is something I originally developed at university with my tutorial partner, Nick Middleton. There is no technique, other than using common sense – the sort that you would expect from a layperson in a pub. If there is a technique, it lies in the brutal simplicity of the questions, and the production of jargon-free answers. By now you should have roughly three piles of paper – one of rivers, one of dams, and one of ballistics. I say piles because you may be running a large, complicated business. If there is a lot of material, you might want to take a while to sort the wheat from the chaff and organize it into easily discernible parts.

Put the river information on the table and stare at it. Ask yourself this question:

- Why do these bits work so well?

Do not rush the answer(s). Write them down. Now apply some common sense analysis with more questions.

- Is that *really* the reason?
- Could it be for other reasons?
- If that is the reason, can I take it and apply it somewhere else in the business?
- Can I think of other possible applications?

From this process, you should be able to generate a highly promising list of ideas that emulate good things that your business already does. In other words, if something is a success, work out why and replicate it elsewhere. Some words of caution here though: always admit if something was a fluke.

Under no circumstances should you come away from this piece of analysis concluding that you should replicate something good elsewhere when you don't actually know why it worked in the first place. Sometimes, things just work through luck. Combinations of factors collide – timing, pricing, packaging, outside factors – to make something work, whether you planned them that way or not. If you were genuinely surprised by the success of something, and are not sure of the reasons behind that success, then admit it. Do not go around pretending that you planned it all along – it will come back to bite you at some point. Just use the good thing to stimulate the next good thing. Use the principle: so that worked – have I got any more good ideas based on that?

Now put the dams on the table. This bit may be less pleasant, but it will be just as instructive. Ask yourself the question:

- Why do these bits not work well?

Write down the answers and again apply common sense analysis by probing with more questions.

- Is that *really* the reason?
- Could it be for other reasons?
- If so, what are they?

- If that is the reason, how can I fix it?
- If I can't fix it, who can?

If you can't see a clear way through it all, don't panic. Grab your ballistics sheet and review the headings.

- **Projectiles:** who, or what, is heading where?
- **Propulsion forces:** who, or what, is making them do that?
- **Aerodynamics:** who, or what, has good momentum behind it?
- **Resistance:** who, or what, is resisting forward motion?
- **Gravity:** is there anything structural that anchors any of this?

Now reorganize the rivers and dams information by the ballistics categories. Use the questions associated with each component to try to unravel how something might be resolved. For example, does a resistance question help solve an issue? Does the gravity of the business explain why something is as it is? Does a propulsion force provide a clue as to how to fix a dam? Here is a full set of examples.

Projectiles

- Are we dealing with a projectile here?
- Who, or what, is heading where?
- Is that good or bad?
- If it's good, how can it be replicated elsewhere?
- If it's bad, how can it be fixed?

Propulsion forces

- Are we dealing with a propulsion force?
- Who, or what, is making them do that?
- Is that good or bad?
- If it's good, how can it be replicated elsewhere?
- If it's bad, how can it be fixed?

Aerodynamics

- Is this to do with aerodynamics?
- Who, or what, has good momentum behind it?
- How can that be harnessed?

Resistance

- Is this a case of resistance?
- Who, or what, is resisting forward motion?
- How can that be fixed?

Gravity

- Is gravity at work here?
- Is there something structural or cultural anchoring this?
- Can that be turned to our advantage or does it need fixing?

'When the facts change, I change my mind. What do you do?'
John Maynard Keynes

Hopefully, this type of cross-examination should be helping to shed any fuzzy thinking. Remember we are still only dealing in the realms of fact. It is your job to face the facts maturely, and see them for what they are. Do not let bias and prejudice creep in to your thinking, and be prepared to change your mind if the facts suggest that it would be a good idea to do so.

'The more you learn the worse things get.' *Mark Twain*

There may be a certain element here of not wanting to face the truth, but you must. Take heart from the fact that all intelligent people and successful businesses learn from mistakes. This is the very essence of all successful evolution. If you are not capable of working out what went wrong and how it could be done better next time, then your business will never evolve. So be reassured that making mistakes is perfectly fine, so long as you are able to identify them accurately, and then take the necessary remedial action.

'Mistakes are the portals of discovery.' *James Joyce*

It was once said that we all make mistakes, and when we have made enough, they call it experience. Do not be afraid of mistakes. They usually lead to something else, particularly if they are absorbed humbly and thoughtfully. Another way of looking at it is that you can't make any mistakes if you don't do anything, and vice versa. If you never cook, you never spill any ingredients on the floor. If you never wash up, you never break any plates. Some form of action with a few flaws is far preferable to inaction.

> **'The man who makes no mistakes does not usually make anything.'** *Edward John Phelps*

Rivers
- Where are the rivers?
- How many of them are there?
- How large?
- How small?
- How many in total?

Dams
- Where are the dams?
- How many of them are there?
- How large?
- How small?
- How many in total?

Ballistics

Projectiles: who, or what, is heading where?
Propulsion forces: who, or what, is making them do that?
Aerodynamics: who, or what, has good momentum behind it?
Resistance: who, or what, is resisting forward motion?
Gravity: is there anything structural that anchors any of this?

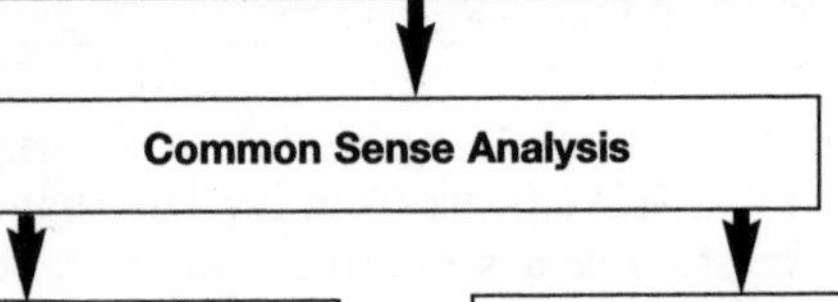

Rivers
- Why do these bits work so well?
- Is that *really* the reason?
- Could it be for other reasons?
- If that is the reason, can I take it and apply it somewhere else in the business?
- If so, can I write a list of other possible applications of this finding?

Dams
- Why do these bits not work well?
- Is that *really* the reason?
- Could it be for other reasons?
- If so, what are they?
- If that is the reason, how can I fix it?
- If I can't fix it, who can?

figure 3 evolutive thinking stage 1: facts

'I've learnt from my mistakes, and I'm sure I can repeat them.' *Peter Cook*

Also be aware that you need to approach your thinking with the right tools for the job. If an issue is highly technical, then you may wish to use this process alongside someone who knows the technical detail, and can therefore answer the majority of the tricky questions that it throws up. There's no point in generating scores of questions that you cannot personally answer, unless it is your specific intent to raise them all, and then go to the experts for their solutions. Far better to embark on the process with an approximate idea of what you think might emerge, and have the necessary people on hand to help you out.

'If all you have is a hammer, everything begins to look like a nail.' *Nietzsche*

Diving in to any wide-ranging thought process without decent preparation is inadvisable. If you embark on it with only one angle, you may only generate the one solution, and it will probably be the same as everything you have come up with before. Most issues have multiple possible solutions, so you need to stay open-minded as to what these might be. This may mean that, if you adopt this evolutive thinking technique, you might want to run it in parallel with another method to see if you emerge with a richer combination of ideas and answers.

'When you have a hammer all problems start to look like a nail. But when you don't have a hammer, you don't want anything to look like a nail.' *Robert Kagan*

I guess Nietzsche made his observation long before Robert Kagan, but his addition to the analogy makes an interesting point. If you embark on some careful thought without any techniques or any shape to organize your thinking, then you may well only emerge with a re-statement of your problems. So try to regard this technique as your hammer, and hit those nails right on the head.

Remind me, what *was* the original idea?

One final point on the Facts stage: if you find yourself getting in a muddle, do stop and ask yourself this fundamental question: What *was* the original idea? It could refer to anything – why you set the business up in the first place, what the vision or purpose of your company is, why you bother to come to work in the morning – anything that is crucial to the matter in hand. The original idea always lies at the heart of what is important. So remind yourself what it was in the first place, and use that as an anchor point to prevent your thoughts from drifting off into weird areas that don't help you on to the next thing.

Chapter 4 recap

1. Have you written out your lists of rivers and dams?
2. Did you analyse them carefully to find out why things are as they are?
3. What did you conclude?
4. Did you try the ballistic questions?
5. What did that reveal?
6. Did you look at your successes to see if they were flukes?
7. Have you worked out how to replicate good things elsewhere?
8. Have you revisited your original idea for the business?
9. How are you going to fix the bad bits?
10. What was the mistake you learnt most from and why?

Cautionary Tale: Daisy Mann, the florist who couldn't let go

Daisy always wanted to be a successful businesswoman, and by the age of 25 she had set up her own florist shop. Things went well, and she built a thriving business. Several years later, she had three children and everything continued to work superbly because she could open late and close early, still do the school run and maintain a really well balanced lifestyle. If earnings were down a little, it didn't matter because the kids were being brought up how she wanted. And it was easy enough getting someone to cover for her occasionally, or just shut up shop to take holidays.

After ten years of this, with the kids increasingly independent, Daisy became bored and decided to expand her operation significantly. She attracted some outside investment, bought another shop, and hired more people. More openings followed, and then she set up a warehousing operation to hold and provide stock. Three years later, she had six shops, a warehouse and 27 staff.

Things seemed to be going brilliantly. The money was pouring in and world domination was proving stimulating. Then one of her best shop managers resigned, citing as his main grievance that Daisy was always meddling and wouldn't allow him any decent autonomy. She wasn't actually allowing him to manage, and in many instances he felt that that her micro-management style bordered on the condescending. Three months later, another manager resigned with similar parting remarks.

Daisy was upset and couldn't work out what had gone wrong. She had dealt with those shops just as she had with the one she started in, understanding every detail and staying fully involved. But that was the whole point. Daisy had failed to change her style of running the business to reflect its new size. She was managing an operation ten times the size as though it were her original shop. In doing so, she had not learned to let go a large proportion of the stuff that she used to do every day.

That is what can happen when you expand. You end up doing lots of things you never did before, and relinquishing many that you do currently. So before you start the expansion, you need to work out what those things are, and decide whether you are braced for the changes that will inevitably follow.

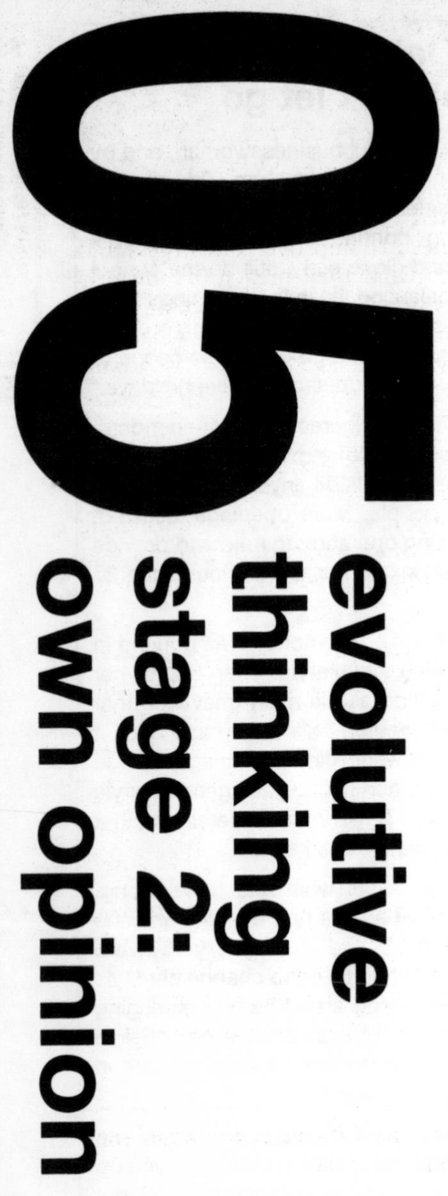

05 evolutive thinking stage 2: own opinion

In this chapter you will learn:

- **how to harness your own opinion**
- **how to heed your own counsel**
- **the drawbacks of not doing so**
- **the difference between scepticism and cynicism**
- **how to be pragmatic, but not to compromise**

The doctor who died of ill health

So you have the facts on the table in front of you. What works, and what doesn't. Now is the time to introduce your opinion to the equation. You will be familiar with the phrase: heed your own counsel. And yet life is full of examples of people who fail to do precisely that. Whether it is true or not, received wisdom suggests that doctors always tell you how to live longer, that smoking is bad, and that you need to improve your fitness and your diet. But do they practice what they preach? Frequently not. Decorators often have tatty houses that need a lick of paint. They don't want to come home and do for themselves what they do all day for a living. And advertising agencies are often poor at promoting themselves, despite the fact that they do it successfully every day for their clients.

So the point is, you give out good advice all day – are you capable of paying attention to your own advice? This is what this section is all about: heeding your own counsel, and listening to your own opinion. This is the time to introduce some of that factual pollution we mentioned in the last chapter. It is time for you to listen to your own opinion.

> **Opinion** (noun): judgement or belief not founded on certainty or proof

The facts will, in the main, speak for themselves, and the nasty home truths certainly will, so don't dwell on those. Now start considering what your perspective on the issues is. If you are conducting this process as part of a strategic rethink with colleagues, then you might want to get them to contribute their opinions too. Just make sure that people don't all dive in with their opinions and prejudices at the beginning. Make sure that stage one has been done first. Then you can evaluate their opinions in the context of the facts, rather than just as a random series of views.

> **'Don't argue for the difficulties. The difficulties will argue for themselves.'** *Winston Churchill*

In the next chapter, we will scrutinize the opinions of 60 or more business people, and one of the recurring themes is that you should always trust your instincts. Up until the mid-1980s, it was normal for people in business to have a hunch and go with it. Then came research, pre-testing, and a range of other techniques for checking if an idea was viable before it ever saw the light of day. For enormous product launches that require multi-million pound investments, that is totally valid. But for simple, ingenious ways of galvanizing your business, it is totally unnecessary. Have a hunch and go for it. If it doesn't work, do something else. It's that simple. In chapter 3, we talked about how the next big thing might be small, and I referred to Malcolm Gladwell's book, *The Tipping Point*. Well, he has since written another book called *Blink*. The central tenet of it is that a snap judgement made very quickly can actually be more effective than one made deliberately and cautiously. He introduces the notion of thin slicing, in which the impression gained of something in the first two seconds is almost always more reliable than one built up over a longer period of time. There is a summary for you in the appendix.

So trust your instincts, and those of respected colleagues. Do not ignore your own counsel and become a doctor who dies of ill health, having failed to listen to your own advice. We will start by dragging your opinions out of you, and then go on to introduce some devil's advocate elements to test-drive those opinions for validity.

Heed your own counsel

Take your sheets of rivers, dams and ballistics, and re-read them. Work through each in turn, asking yourself these questions. Remember to heed your own counsel.

- What do I *personally* think of this issue?
- What does my colleague think?
- If it's a bad thing, do I know how to fix it?
- If it's a good thing, how can I develop it?
- What is my immediate thought about what to do next?

Write down the answers to these and put them on one side. Now start making some decisions. If an idea is rubbish, throw it away. By now, some of the ideas will have bitten the dust, and those that remain on the table are probably pretty robust. Review what is left and, if necessary, write them out again because they may have taken a bit of a battering on the way. It is worthwhile taking the time to do this because scribbled ideas with too many comments on them are often confusing. Ideally, an idea should consist of one word or one sentence. If expressed that simply, it is much easier to determine whether it is going to work or not. Only ever put one idea on one piece of paper, so as not to confuse or interlink any of them. Chuck away all the old scribbles and go off and do something different. If you have been at it for a while, take a breather or come back to it tomorrow. So, to recap, you should now have just one pile of paper, each with one idea on it, expressed either as one sentence or, better still, one word.

The pragmatist who was sceptical about the cynic

Now we are going to introduce the devil's advocate, or the devil's avocado as an old colleague always used to say. As you know, that is an opposing, and often unpopular, view and in business these can take various forms. For the sake of this evolutive thinking process, I have chosen two views: sceptical and cynical. Once we have examined these in detail, we will counterbalance them with a healthy dose of pragmatism.

Let's start at the sharp end. A cynic is someone who thinks the worst of almost every person or situation. At their most extreme, they are no fun to have around. Sometimes they are called killers, because they only ever kill ideas and they never seem to have any themselves.

> **Cynic** (noun): a person who believes the worst about people or the outcome of events

As a personality trait, therefore, cynicism is not very desirable, but as an aid to rational thought, it can be very helpful in sorting out which ideas are good and which are lousy. Hundreds of years ago, a cynic was a member of a sect founded by a guy called Antisthenes. These people scorned worldly things and believed that self-control was the key to the only good available in the world. A pretty heavy notion I'm sure you'll agree, but that's by the by. For our purposes, a short, sharp blast of cynicism will sort the wheat from the chaff, the good ideas from the not-so-good. As the saying goes, the good is the enemy of the great. In fact, some people are active fans of cynicism, and believe it is as close as you can get to truly accurate observation.

'The power of accurate observation is often called cynicism by those who do not have it.' *George Bernard Shaw*

So we are going to cross-examine our ideas with a set of cynical questions. You might think that this approach is a bit strange, but there is a method behind the madness. You have probably come across Edward de Bono's system of putting on different coloured hats to represent different character types and ways of thinking. Well, this is similar, but you can do it on your own. It forces you to adopt frames of mind that you wouldn't usually consider if left to your own devices and, crucially, it enables you to replicate the possible reactions of colleagues and customers to the new ideas. So the next part of this stage is to ask a series of cynical questions. Here we go.

- What's the point of that?
- That will never work, will it?
- That didn't work before so it won't work now, will it?
- They'll never go for that, will they?
- How can we afford that?
- No one is going to buy that, are they?

I haven't gone on and on with a long list, because the negative nature of these questions is quite draining. Don't overdo it, just briefly adopt the position of someone who cannot see a way through for the proposed idea. It will rapidly reveal whether the initiative can withstand aggressive scrutiny.

Now we are going to move on to a milder line of enquiry, basing it on scepticism.

Originally a sceptic was a member of one of the ancient Greek schools of philosophy, populated by people like Pyrrho, who believed that real knowledge of things is impossible. Another rather weighty philosophical thought, but again, not one that should put us off much. Sceptics aren't saying no to something, they just aren't convinced. What they want is more proof that something is likely to work. There is a lovely moment in a book called *The Pirate Inside*, by Adam Morgan. In it, he describes the personal characteristics that make individuals in companies agitate for change. When interviewing Bob Gill of Pringles, he asks him what his reaction is whenever someone says no to an idea. 'Oh,' he says, 'you basically treat the word no as a request for further information.' How brilliant is that? Ever the optimist, lively bright people in business believe so much in their ideas that they just keep going until everybody else says yes. So consider this sceptical element of the evolutive thinking process as a request for further verification that the idea in question does indeed have merit.

Sceptical (adjective): not convinced that something is true; tending to mistrust people and ideas

Go back to your pile of ideas, and subject them to some further interrogation.

- How will that work then?
- Will it be viable?
- Will people be impressed by it?
- Will it complement the current business well?
- Can the idea be pushed even further?
- Are there even more possibilities beyond that?

It doesn't matter in what order you ask these questions, nor whether you ask the cynical set before or after this sceptical set. The important thing is that you have embarked on some form of elimination process. This will ensure that you don't waste time later pursuing ideas when you could already have worked out for yourself that they probably wouldn't work anyway.

'If one regards oneself as a sceptic, it is as well from time to time to be sceptical about one's scepticism.' *Freud*

Round three takes the pragmatist's perspective. This is where we survey the two extreme sets of opinions and draw them together to strike some sort of sensible balance. This is not the same as killing a perfectly good idea. It is sense-checking the likelihood of something actually getting done.

Pragmatism (noun): the doctrine that the content of a concept consists only in its practical applicability

An idea is only as good as your ability to enact it, so what we now need is a pragmatic check. Review the ideas asking these questions.

- Can you afford it?
- Have you got the resources to implement it?
- Will customers and colleagues accept it?
- Have you got the time to do it?

Death to compromise

You should be down to a highly manageable number by now, so all that is left is a reality check and some fine-tuning. Pause for a minute or, as a colleague of mine used to say, stand back and take a closer look. This is the point at which you need to agree if you are happy to go public with the ideas. There is no room for compromise here. You are either going to do it, or you are not.

- Is there any element of bluff or self-delusion in it?
- Is it a forced fit or does it sit comfortably with everything else?
- Could it be better articulated?
- Is it free of jargon?
- Can you relate to it?
- Will other people?
- Are you happy to go public with it?

Compromise (noun): settlement by concessions on both sides; something midway between two or more different things

That's pretty much it. Just don't compromise the idea or how you are going to execute it. Remember: you are either going to do it, or you are not. Be decisive, and get ready to enact it.

'Consensus is when we have a discussion. They tell me what they think. Then I decide.' *Lee Iacocca*

Heed your own counsel

- What do I personally think of this issue?
- What does my colleague think?
- If it's a bad thing, do I know how to fix it?
- If it's a good thing, how can I develop it?
- What is my immediate thought about what to do next?

Sceptical view

- How will that work then?
- Will it be viable?
- Will people be impressed by it?
- Will it complement the current business well?
- Can the idea be pushed even further?
- Are there even more possibilities beyond that?

Cynical view

- What's the point of that?
- That will never work, will it?
- That didn't work before so it won't work now, will it?
- They'll never go for that, will they?
- How can we afford that?
- No one is going to buy that, are they?

Pragmatic check

- Can you afford it?
- Have you got the resources to implement it?
- Will customers and colleagues accept it?
- Have you got the time to do it?

Compromise check

- Is there any element of bluff or self-delusion in it?
- Is it a forced fit or does it sit comfortably with everything else?
- Could it be better articulated?
- Is it free of jargon?
- Can you relate to it?
- Will other people?
- Are you happy to go public with it?

figure 4 evolutive thinking stage 2: own opinion

This chapter was all about coming to decisions. You have covered a lot of ground now, so it is time to pause and reflect. You should have taken the facts, and overlaid your own opinion. If that was a bit wishy-washy in places, the cynical or sceptical view should have helped to crystallize your opinion, so that you could reach a consensus with yourself. You should have ended up with one clear pile of ideas, rigorously sense-checked for their practicability. In a way, therefore, you are ready to enact them, and if you feel completely confident in them, then do go ahead and do that now. If you are still anxious, discuss them with a colleague. If you don't have anyone of that type, or even if you would value a second opinion, you might want to look at the next chapter. It contains a vast amount of other people's wisdom.

Chapter 5 recap

1. Have you heeded your own counsel?
2. Have you trusted your instincts?
3. Did you adopt the cynical position?
4. Did that force you to reject some ideas?
5. Did you pose the sceptical questions?
6. Have you overcome those reservations or clarified things as a result?
7. What did the pragmatic check reveal?
8. Have you compromised at all in any of this?
9. Are you ready to go public with the ideas?
10. Have you paused to reflect on progress so far?

Success Story: Gordon Allman, the television producer who realized that the 'next big thing' could be small

Success is relative. Growth may or may not matter. It depends what you want from life, and how much you feel the need to tell anyone who will listen how wonderfully successful you are, and how fast your supposedly amazing business is growing.

Gordon began life as a television producer in a top ten advertising agency in their heyday in the 1980s and 1990s, enjoying top pay and budgets that often stretched to millions of pounds. Technology and a couple of recessions changed all that. Fast forward twenty years and clients would expect to pay £30,000 for a commercial rather than ten times the amount, and technology made it happen much faster, often missing out layers of human expertise.

Many high-ranking producers left the industry, retired to Spain or retreated to Devon to write their long-promised novel. Not Gordon. He was convinced that there was still mileage in the tank, and didn't see any reason why he shouldn't be able to apply his experience to the industry even though budgets had shrunk and the technology had moved on.

He investigated all the permutations thoroughly. Researching the new technology was not difficult – it just took an inquisitive mind and some proper thinking time. Designing a business model that would work on the reduced budgets was more of a challenge, but it definitely could be done. He calculated that he could have a decent life by doing two jobs a month, with an average budget of £30,000 and a margin of 20 per cent, so that's how he started, positioning himself as 'big company experience in a small package' (he wasn't that tall, which helped with the banter too).

Gordon was a success because he was able to adapt to changing market conditions. He subsumed his ego and got on with designing the next thing. Once he had established his proposition and cut his cloth accordingly, he was able to build a thriving business, always working on the principle that the next big thing might be small.

06 evolutive thinking stage 3: other people's wisdom

In this chapter you will learn other people's answers to six fascinating questions:

1. **what is the hardest thing about growing your business?**
2. **is growth always a good thing?**
3. **did you ever suffer from post-launch blues or a three-year itch?**
4. **how do you plan the 'next big thing'?**
5. **if you could have known one thing when you started that you know now, what would it be?**
6. **is there anything else you would like to pass on about growing or evolving your business?**

Stage three of the evolutive thinking process is drawing upon the wisdom of others. This is not so much a process as a bit of osmosis. All business people are fascinated by the experiences of others, so here we collect a wide range of opinions and try to organize them in such a way as to help you develop your own business. This is very much a do-it-yourself chapter. If you are particularly interested in one question, go straight to it to see the answers. If you are interested in a certain size of business, look at all those answers. If you aspire to being larger than your current size of business, then look at the answers given by the businesses that are larger than yours, in order to see the sorts of issues they face.

The survey explained

The survey asked those running businesses of all types six questions:

1 What is the hardest thing about growing your business?
2 Is growth always a good thing?
3 Did you ever suffer from post-launch blues or a three-year itch?
4 How do you plan the 'next big thing'?
5 If you could have known one thing when you started that you know now, what would it be?
6 Is there anything else you would like to pass on about growing or evolving your business?

As well as adding my own interpretation of the responses, the answers are grouped by company size to enable you to go straight to the views of those who run businesses of your size, or the size you think you want to be. They are divided into:

- Sole traders
- Small partnerships (two or three people)
- Fewer than 10 staff
- 10–50 staff
- More than 50 staff

I should stress at this stage that this is not a quantitative survey. It is totally qualitative and it is not statistically significant. So no attempt is made to assert claims such as 'x per cent of sole traders agree that growth is a good thing'. What we are interested in is the broad sweep of opinion, and frequently with the contradictions and dilemmas that are revealed. The responses to each question are followed by an initial diagnosis and, once we have looked at all the answers to a particular question, there is an overall diagnosis and verdict.

'Wisdom is the reward you receive for a lifetime of listening when you'd rather have been talking.' *Aristotle*

In summarizing these points, I have let the respondents in the main speak for themselves, because the advice they give is clear in its own right, and requires no further explanation from me. After working through this for the six questions, we have a huge bank of wisdom from which to draw, so at the very end of the chapter, I try to bring some of the strands together. All the advice is then included in a manifesto for growing your business – 110 pieces of other people's wisdom.

The six questions answered

These are all extracts, drawn together in order to summarize the main debating points for each question. If you want to look at the full responses of any particular individual, choose your business category by staff number and go to the appendix. Right, let's dive in and see what people had to say. The first question is designed to get to the crux of what people find difficult when it comes to growing their business.

Question 1: What is the hardest thing about growing your business?

Sole traders

- Gaining, developing and maintaining those important and useful contacts.
- Staying focused.
- The lack of hours in a day.
- Brainstorming new ideas is difficult.
- In the early stages, there is a great deal of unused time. Much of the problem is boredom, which can be demoralizing. The key is using that time effectively to secure new business and

to banish guilt. If you cannot contribute to your new business effort with an additional hour's work then take the kids to a museum or go for a walk – it will be better for you in the long run.

- Keeping motivation high as it is easy to slip into a routine.
- Keeping motivated. If you have no problems with inclination, and are convinced that your commercial pursuit is the best thing you could be doing with your life (rather than, say, taking the kids swimming more or spending a day a week on the novel/photography course/etc.) – and that having more of whatever it brings would definitely be worth the effort – then you'll find the time to make those calls, put in the strategic thinking time, pitch that extension to your usual remit. If not, it will appear that the hardest thing is finding the time, but that will be nonsense.
- Making new sales and developing the product at the same time as servicing the growing base of existing clients, suppliers etc. Finding the time and energy for recruitment and then training of new staff – it's hard to take the financial risk of hiring ahead of the curve but it's very easy then to find yourself 'too busy to delegate'.
- Converting interest into income.
- Increasing the price tag of my outputs (while not wanting to increase the number of employees from 1 to 1+).
- Patience.
- Deciding how much control to cede. I'm still in the early stages of setting up a new business but am already facing tough decisions about growth. The hardest decision for me is how much control to cede in my new company in the pursuit of growth through partnership working. I have been approached by a much larger brand in my sector to form a partnership and must negotiate cannily to maintain my independence and build my fledgling brand.

Initial diagnosis

- Work hard on motivation
- Be patient
- Keep a close eye on time pressures
- Nurture contacts carefully

Small partnerships (two or three people)

- Bringing in the additional revenue that creates growth. Managing growth is not easy but generating the extra sales and profit is the hardest part. To be able to do this successfully you need a good market positioning, good marketing, good selling technique and good negotiating. You obviously then need to deliver the goods or services consistently at a high quality level.
- Moving from working with clients you want to work with to being stuck with selling the organization.
- Finding the right balance between going after new business and smothering your existing clients in love and attention.
- Taking a risk, trusting that your judgement and abilities will sustain any growth.
- In our case it's been working around all the legal restrictions which have been tough due to restrictive covenants.
- Taking the plunge, anxiety about the consequences: risk, responsibility, staff, salaries, technology and financing it all.
- The hardest thing about growing your business is letting go and involving other people – collaboration is the key to success.

Initial diagnosis

- Take the plunge and take risks
- Learn to let go of some things
- Use your partners judiciously

Fewer than 10 staff

- The single largest challenge is overcoming the 'Nobody ever got fired for hiring IBM' phenomenon. Customers embrace the notion of change, but when faced with taking the radical step of doing something new and different, risk aversion creeps in. As a consequence, the second largest challenge becomes finding customers brave enough to act upon their disillusionment or disappointment with the status quo, and to do something about it.
- I don't want my business to get too big – I had severe cash flow problems years ago. The tricky thing is finding the balance – approaching new clients to maintain the client and

income level in balance, without over-stretching yourself both in terms of staffing and outgoings. I try to find a level where we give new and current clients the attention they need, whilst keeping an ear to the ground for new opportunities in case one project terminates suddenly or a client goes under.

- For me, I have a huge desire not only to keep our overheads to a minimum, and also not to have the responsibility of staff to think about. Luckily, we are in a business whereby we can employ people on a job for job basis, which means their fees are covered.
- Maintaining a focus on new business whilst delivering high quality work to existing customers – especially when you are busy and expanding 'organically' within your existing customer base. Oh yes, and getting the timing right when expanding capacity.
- The hardest thing is taking the decision to grow and be responsible for the costs of people, plant and premises. Working for yourself you can pretty much take the salary that you want, but when you take on a team, you have to make sure that they come first, that they are paid first, motivated, that they take their holidays. By taking the decision to grow – make sure you have the right team around you to facilitate the growth and that they come up to your expectations.
- Developing a client base that will pay a market rate for your time.
- Committing to the inevitable increase in overhead.
- Bureaucracy, cash flow and time.

Initial diagnosis

- Find brave customers
- Grow prudently
- Keep an eye on escalating bureaucracy

10–50 staff

- Choosing the correct strategic direction to take and being able to implement it. You need to have a clear understanding of why your business exists and what it is good at. If this is understood and believed in internally, it becomes much easier to communicate externally and more attractive to potential new clients.

- Risking what you have built up so far.
- Finding and keeping the right people.
- Identifying the right person, or people, that will help you make it happen.
- The arbitrary nature of growth – often knowing where to put the effort in as so often the results come back where you least expect it. Having the commitment to prioritize properly and not simply trying to do more of everything less well rather than identifying the right strategy and backing it.
- Finding the right people. Whether small or large, today no one in your organization is 'invisible' and you can't take risks for long. Our business is differentiated largely by the quality of our strategic input and intelligence and to take on someone who doesn't represent this is dangerous (tried once and burnt fingers). Also, ensuring that you are not just different to your competition, but ahead of the game. Working out what is going to be the next issue. We spend a lot on marketing intelligence, trends and information.
- I guess it depends what your forte is. For me, staff management. Two, three, four staff no problem. Once we went from 10 to say 15, we found we needed much more formal processes to keep everyone on board and trying to achieve the same thing. Also it seems to be very easy to spend time managing staff rather than concentrating on the really important things.
- After winning the first few contracts, finding the right people to expand the work.
- Being in the right shape to capitalize on opportunities.
- Saving today's income for tomorrow's expansion.
- The main challenge is finding the right staff. It is important that a business retains its 'can do' culture and therefore hiring the right team is vitally important as otherwise it is impossible to grow because the management becomes a bottleneck.
- Finding the time to dream, review, plan and then stick with it.
- I'm not an entrepreneur and therefore find it difficult to comment on a lot of the specifics. However one overall belief that I have about growth is that 'you don't have to win by much to win by a lot'. The issue is that of the virtues of compound growth. Consider two scenarios:

    1 If you can grow a business by 5 per cent for ten years rather than 2 per cent (i.e two and half times as fast) you will end up with three times the additional sales ... and

probably more than three times the incremental profit and much enhanced exit multiple.

2 Steady growth at, say, 5 per cent for ten years is better than four years growth at 15 per cent per annum, then stasis or decline.

- Getting the right staff for the right money.
- Balancing the need for structure, process and systems with the requirement to keep the fleet-footedness of the start-up.
- Different skills required to set up a business as opposed to grow a business. Entrepreneurs have skills to set up, but this doesn't mean they have those for growth such as leadership, strategy, systems and controls, finance skills. The difficult bit is identifying talent to bring these skills in – if we don't have the skills how can we effectively select people who do? For example, interviewing finance directors is extremely difficult!
- If you have been used to running a large and well-known company previously, then it's recognising that a new set of rules apply to growing a smaller firm. It's harder as, to begin with, the name recognition isn't there and you have to be twice as good as the opposition to be perceived as doing as good a job.

Initial diagnosis

- Spend the time to find the right people
- Realize that different skills are required to set up a business as opposed to grow one
- You don't have to win by much to win by a lot
- Save today's income for tomorrow's expansion
- Have a clear understanding of why your business exists

More than 50 staff

- Balancing the often conflicting objectives that the new business process throws up. Under usual circumstances we very much believe in making the right recommendation to solve the client's business or communications problem. In a pitch the objective is to win. These two are not the same thing.
- Getting real scale.
- Managing the transition in terms of people, process and profit. Maintaining standards and culture. Keeping ahead of

the game in terms of investment and strategic change. Avoiding going after everything that moves. Having a clear proposition.

- Quality organic revenue growth. It is my view that we should not acquire businesses in the same market as ourselves to increase our customer base. We should have good enough people to win the business and grow it organically as it is. You should only acquire businesses to add skill sets you do not already have. Getting the quality people who can develop and add new accounts is the hardest thing.
- Finding the time to invest in growth because this time earns me money tomorrow yet my staff and shareholders need to be paid today.
- Building the right team.
- Having the right people in the right place at the appropriate time in the growth/size of the business. Someone who is fantastic at the start can be out of their depth later on – and not recognize the fact.
- That too much growth is predicated on trying to win new business. The willing diversion of your best people – for free, for several weeks at a time – from your paying clients and best (organic growth) prospects.
- Remembering that you have a family and a private life and being a workaholic is boring for the people who might meet you whether through work or outside of work. If you're not an interesting person, people won't want to do business with you. Keep true to you, 'the person', don't become 'the business'.
- In a service business the servicing of current clients takes total precedence. Therefore dedicating resource to future business is often put on the backburner. The result is many businesses hit a glass ceiling of revenue and can't break through to the next level. It is very difficult to take the hard decision and divide the senior team into today and tomorrow.
- Managing the demands of new business, whilst keeping existing clients happy.
- Finding people with the necessary passion and talent to ensure the culture and style of the company doesn't get diluted.

Initial diagnosis

- Avoid going after everything that moves
- Only acquire businesses to add skill sets you do not already have
- Find the time to invest in growth
- Build the right team
- If you're not an interesting person, people won't want to do business with you

Question 1: What is the hardest thing about growing your business?

Overall diagnosis and verdict: How to develop your business successfully

- Have a clear understanding of why your business exists
- Work hard on motivation
- Be patient
- Keep a close eye on time pressures
- Nurture contacts carefully
- Take the plunge and take risks
- Learn to let go of some things
- Use your partners judiciously
- Find brave customers
- Grow prudently
- Keep an eye on escalating bureaucracy
- Spend the time to find the right people and build the right team
- Remember different skills are required to set up a business than to grow one
- You don't have to win by much to win by a lot
- Save today's income for tomorrow's expansion
- Avoid going after everything that moves
- Only acquire businesses to add skill sets you do not already have
- Find the time to invest in growth
- If you're not an interesting person, people won't want to do business with you

Question 2: Is growth always a good thing?

The second question is intended to flush out whether everybody thinks growth is good, and, if not, what is preferable?

Sole traders

- Yes, as long as quality of service is maintained.
- No, there's good growth and bad growth. In the early days bad growth is doing things for money when you should be doing it for your reputation.
- No – being true to yourself and your ideals is better.
- Growth has many forms. One could call reducing company staff and company expenses growth, if the company were to have a better bottom line figure. Sometimes growth can be time spent learning not to make the same mistakes.
- I have always read that growing quicker than the capacity the business can handle can be catastrophic because cash flow and production problems scupper any future benefit. However, I also think growth can take you off course. I think you need to bear in mind what you started the business for and make sure you grow in that direction.
- Growth is always a good thing if it is what you planned for. If you don't have a contingency plan in place for sudden expansion opportunities, the way you handle growth could be your downfall. Luckily, small businesses in the UK have the opportunity to tap into a great network of contacts making it much easier to pull in skills and support needed to deal effectively and professionally with growth when your company is not quite aligned to deal with the extra commitment.
- Revenue and profit growth is always a good thing. Bowing to clients' pressure to take on staff or additional staff is something that needs to be thought about extremely carefully. It's important to have a clear understanding of how much money one wants to extract from the business over a certain time period. It may be that staying as small as possible may achieve that net profit goal whereas staff growth may destroy it completely.
- Absolutely not. Keeping up with inflation is good, any more than that is optional. There's a lot to be said for ticking over and sleeping well.

- Depends why you set up in business in the first place. If you want to become wealthy beyond your wildest dreams then growth is probably at least usually good, so long as it's profitable. If, however, you are more interested in autonomy or creativity or some non-financial measure then growth could be your worst enemy – at some point you will be spending all your time managing staff and/or investors rather than engaging in your chosen business.
- No, but I'd generally prefer to be troubled by excessive growth than none at all.
- Certainly not. Too many people are too obsessed with growth as a mantra. Your next book should be called 'Teach Yourself Evolving your Business'. Greater profit always sounds nice but at what cost in other departments? Remember the difference between price and value.

Initial diagnosis

- There is good growth and bad growth
- Bad growth is doing things for the wrong reasons
- Growth is good so long as it is profitable
- Growth usually involves making a lot of mistakes
- Work out how much money you want to extract and over what time period
- Make sure quality of service is maintained

Small partnerships (two or three people)

- I do not think growth should be for growth's sake. Growth should mean bigger profits (more than enough to justify the extra hassle that growth brings) and not just size.
- No. Then again, if you don't grow you're stuck selling the one service or product that you or a very small team can deliver.
- Yes. Customers come and go. Your business is a leaky bucket, which needs to be topped up constantly. You have to be careful to manage your growth though or, perversely, it might bankrupt you.
- You have to weigh up what's most important: a) a higher turnover with more business which is likely to help attract more clients and good employees but might be less profitable and harder to manage if achieved too soon; or b) a tighter ship with better margins and therefore profit, but which

looks, initially, less impressive. This is one of our year one challenges.

- Not sure ... but the reason for our hesitancy in going ahead with it is doubtless because deep down we believe indeed it is not!
- Yes. It may not always be comfortable, but it's better than the alternative. If businesses don't grow they die, or grow stagnant. Growth is vital for business and it's up to each business to manage the challenge it represents.

Initial diagnosis

- Do not pursue growth for growth's sake
- Be careful to manage your growth
- Top up your leaky bucket constantly
- Differentiate between higher turnover and better margin

Fewer than 10 staff

- Not necessarily. Controlled and planned growth is, but knowing when to turn down business is an important lesson to learn.
- No. We do not aim to be large and available. Rapid growth endangers quality and reputation. Safe growth keeps your clients as advocates. Our objective is never to have more than ten staff.
- Growth is only a good thing if you can trust the people around you to exceed your own expectations and take the pressure off you as an individual. There is little point in growing if you are clearing up after them and you don't feel like you can delegate.
- As far as I am concerned growth is not always a good thing. I started my own business because I enjoy what I do – I love the fact that if it's a sunny day I can let the staff go early on a Friday or have my god-daughter over to play at work, without upsetting anyone. If the business got too big you get into all sorts of 'political' situations – staffing, training, more dealings with my bank manager – I'd be running a company, not doing work I enjoy.
- I think growth can be a good thing, and perhaps done in stepping stones, and closely monitored and managed to ensure productivity and not waste occurring.

- Not unless it is planned, controlled and cost effective. The desire for turnover is a false goal unless profit follows. The mantra is turnover is vanity, profit is sanity.
- Literal answer – no. But it is always a good thing to consider it.
- Hmm ... maybe, maybe not. Depends if it's at the expense of what your customers buy into and if it stretches your cash flow. For example, as a high-end consultant where people buy into 'you' then will they buy into someone else? What happens if you get a bad patch and they're on your payroll?
- Growth is never a good thing – it's either a great thing or a disastrous thing. If growth is properly managed and does not compromise what you set out to achieve in the first place, great! If it is properly managed and you can live with the consequences of the changes to what you set out to achieve in the first place, great again. But if growth is not properly managed and/or you are uncomfortable with the changes you need to make to accommodate growth, then chances are things are going to go horribly wrong. Somewhere here there is a tie to the famous Bill Bernbach quote of, 'A principle isn't a principle until it costs you money'. That said, there are two things that are worse than growth – standing still, and worse, going backwards.

Initial diagnosis

- Rapid growth can endanger quality and reputation
- Control and plan your growth
- Know when to turn down business
- A principle isn't a principle until it costs you money
- Turnover is vanity, profit is sanity
- Do not compromise what you set out to achieve in the first place

10–50 staff

- Not if it changes the thing about your business that most clients liked. Branding even for small business is crucial. If your first ten clients all picked you for being small and allowed you a good margin to give them a personal service, when they depart and you acquire your thirty-fifth client (who is no longer allowing you that margin), you may find yourself much worse off, closer to no margin and unable to sell yourself as anything but 'medium'.

- Yes. No one thing ever remains the same. To stay as you are is impossible. Just as we as people need to 'grow', so does business.
- Always and at any cost, no. I guess it depends what you want to achieve. I think it is hard to stand still, so I would always go for growth, be it increasing turnover or maintaining turnover but increasing profitability.
- No, it can dilute the quality of the offer to existing clients, which can in turn destroy the business.
- Yes – standing still is certain death.
- Not always but mostly. Growth has to be in line with the strategic aims of the organization. If not, then those aims are diluted. Equally, growth should be a consequence of doing what you do well, rather than a central aim of the company in itself. In the latter instance, there is a strong risk of alienating your current customer base by over concentration on new customer acquisition. However, if managed properly, growth provides the ability to enhance the service that you offer to your current user base, as well as develop your people and give a greater breadth to your scope for managing the development of the business.
- Yes, if the integrity of your product or service doesn't suffer.
- If growth is too rapid it will negatively impact on the business as quality suffers. However, it is impossible to stand still. You are either growing or shrinking so steady growth is always a good thing!
- Yes – without growth there is no ambition, and without ambition I believe you slide backwards.
- No, profit is. If the two are managed well, then yes.
- Depends on the type of business. In a service business you should only grow as fast as your ability to pass on the culture and way of doing things to new people. Grow too fast and you dilute what enabled you to grow in the first place.
- Depends on your lifestyle objectives. If you want a comfortable living and low stress then growth is probably not top of the agenda. Growth is good if it brings stability and certainty to a business. Thereafter the desire for growth from a wealth, ego or power perspective must be weighed up against the negatives in terms of stress, skills to achieve, and overall complexity of life it brings with it.

- No, not if it takes you away from being the type of business you intend to be. You have to turn away the 'wrong' sort of opportunities and that's not always easy.

Initial diagnosis

- Don't change the thing that most clients like
- Don't grow too fast and dilute what enabled you to grow in the first place
- To stay as you are is impossible
- Avoid being 'medium'

More than 50 staff

- No not always. Sometimes small, swift and smart is beautiful and it helps to stick to the knitting rather than getting lost in offering too many services that are neither profitable nor rewarding in the product sense.
- Only if you are prepared to accept the structural implications, including for your own role. The larger the company becomes, the more you have to let others do for you. This is not always easy for a control freak. It is also not good if you are growing in areas you are not expert in. You'll be found out eventually and it'll cost you dearly in time, money and, worst of all, reputation.
- Only if it is profitable. Many businesses view growth as being measured in terms of increase in revenue. This is particularly true in service sector businesses, which tend to have league tables based on turnover. There is no point in taking on projects if it is not cost effective to work them. You can see plenty of businesses who show a percentage increase in revenue outstripping the increase in profitability (in some cases, turnover goes up, profit goes down). I have two recent examples where we have actually walked away from the final stage of a pitch because what we were being asked to do for the money just did not make sense. Revenue is vanity, profit is sanity.
- By and large, yes. I think it is certainly better than the opposite. It is possible to think of examples where companies appear to have grown too fast or grown in a way which conflicts with their founding ethos, but I think this is about the quality of the management rather than the volume of business.

- Not unless it has margin associated with it and is synergistic with whatever the current core business is. In the early start of a company there are often not all the systems and processes in place, and this leads to more hands on. There is probably a model of higher costs, pruning costs, followed by growth again.
- Yes. No growth means no attraction or retention of good people. Decide from the outset whether you want to grow the business – and on what scale.
- If you're trying to build a business for the short-term (i.e. a quick exit) then yes. If you're trying to build a brand and/or culture of more permanence, then you can grow too fast. The wrong customers, the wrong results can set you back a long way in a business.
- No, profit is a good thing. Growth doesn't necessarily matter. You can reward people and also develop new areas of the business if you are profitable. Growth is good and it offers people career paths etc., but it's a complete fallacy that money isn't everything. Money talks and people want to be financially rewarded well.
- Yes, definitely. All businesses are a leaky bucket, income draining out of the hole in the bottom. There has to be a mentality of growth otherwise every business will stall. A good discipline is to assume 10 per cent minimum of income will evaporate in the next year, but target 20 per cent growth giving a new business target of 30 per cent incremental income. This sharpens the mind and will probably deliver 15 per cent growth.
- Not always, but it keeps morale high and new opportunities and challenges to keep us fresh and on our toes.
- No! Momentum is important but size in and of itself is frequently a two-edged sword.

Initial diagnosis

- Momentum is important but size in itself is not
- Adopt a mentality of growth, even if you are not growing
- Revenue is vanity. Profit is sanity

Question 2: Is growth always a good thing?

Overall diagnosis and verdict: The guide to growth

- To stay as you are is impossible
- Momentum is important but size in itself is not
- Adopt a mentality of growth
- There is good growth and bad growth
- Bad growth is doing things for the wrong reasons
- Growth is good so long as it is profitable
- Growth usually involves making a lot of mistakes
- Work out how much money you want to extract and over what time period
- Make sure quality of service is maintained
- Do not pursue growth for growth's sake
- Be careful to manage, control and plan your growth
- Top up your leaky bucket constantly
- Differentiate between higher turnover and better margin
- Rapid growth can endanger quality and reputation
- Know when to turn down business
- A principle isn't a principle until it costs you money
- Turnover or revenue is vanity, profit is sanity
- Do not compromise what you set out to achieve in the first place
- Don't change the thing that most clients like
- Don't grow too fast and dilute what enabled you to grow in the first place
- Avoid being 'medium'

Question 3: Did you ever suffer from post-launch blues or a three-year itch?

The third question is all about motivation. The three-year reference was intentionally specific, and many respondents gave their own time spans.

Sole traders

- Yes. Life as a professional musician can be a rollercoaster ride at the best of times.
- Yes – it's horrible.
- Yes, but at seven years. I sold up both times.
- Post-launch definitely, in that as the company evolves you realize that you and your partners have to evolve along with it, and change mindsets about lots of things from operations to strategy.
- Yes! We live in and are part of a society that forever wants more. Our dreams and wants are continually expanding. On a personal note, I've been building a new company website and in writing out where the company is right now, I realized I've already clearly surpassed all my initial expectations, but hey, my initial expectations aren't what I want now. Itchy times in a company are good, as it makes you continually reassess.
- Yes. Sometimes overwhelmed by the extent of things to manage, other times depressed by the lack of business. But all in all, nothing a bit of mental rationalizing won't take care of.
- Yes – I think this is very common because entrepreneurs are often good 'starters' or 'creators' but poor at routine.
- Being still new to the world of the entrepreneur I have yet to itch. However, my first promotional activity gave me a huge confidence problem. You tend to forget that your business is not as important to your prospects as it is to you. Your new venture is like a new child – you want everyone to say it's a beauty. If the response is anything less, then the resulting post-natal depression can make you take your eye off what's important. I also think it only natural that there is a low after a launch as your focus becomes more rational. You need to see a launch very much as the beginning of the beginning rather than the end of the beginning.
- Three-month! No but seriously. It has to keep transforming into a shinier, newer version of itself, which mine tends to do every nine months or so. Then I have a rubbish three months and then something positive happens, apparently out of the blue but there's no such thing as pure luck, and I'm back in the saddle again.
- Definitely had post-launch blues, but can't comment on a three-year itch.

- Personally no, but those around you who love you most will suffer because they care about you deeply, but for very good reasons you have to keep them a certain distance from developments. Do not let them ride the emotional rollercoaster with you, however often and strenuously they plead.

Initial diagnosis

- You and your partners have to evolve along with your business
- Continually reassess everything
- Keep transforming it into a shinier, newer version of itself
- Entrepreneurs are often good 'starters' or 'creators' but poor at routine
- Regard a launch as the beginning of the beginning rather than the end of the beginning

Small partnerships (two or three people)

- Yup – after about a month. We had client number one but number two was very hard to get. It can be very demoralizing, as can working semi on your own when you've always been used to a big team within a lively environment. Creating a more structured environment and giving myself credit for what I'd already achieved really helped.
- Yes, it's not all a bed of roses; there are highs and lows in business, you have to be able to deal with them both.
- No, can honestly say we didn't. Every year new accounts have come on board and after three years we moved to new offices, which was new and exciting.
- No, but then I've never been one to be depressed.
- We've only been going two years, so I'm still thoroughly enjoying the novelty of working for myself.

Initial diagnosis

- Work out how to deal with the highs and lows in business
- Create a more structured environment
- Give yourself credit for what you have already achieved

Fewer than 10 staff

- Is the Pope Catholic? Does a monk take a drink now and then? I can't believe that anyone would ever answer 'No' to this – or if they do, that they're telling the truth. Once the immediacy of the launch is over, the feeling is similar to that of having completed a new business presentation – an immediate high, followed by a lowness until the next high comes along. You cannot be on a high 100 per cent of the time – at least not legally – and hence there is always going to be a period of 'bluesiness' that follows. As regards the 'three-year itch', can I get back to you in two-and-a-half years?
- When everything went wrong a few years ago I did question what I was doing and if I should go and do something else – but this presents so many challenges, and starting all over again was the biggest. I'm lucky no day is ever the same and as I'm my own boss if I decide to take the company in a slightly different direction we do – it stops the boredom setting in.
- We get involved with planning special memorable occasions such as weddings and it's very exciting and privileged. I have received many texts from brides on honeymoon!
- No, but you do need to take holidays and switch the phone off.
- Like any job you want to move on to doing the next best thing, inevitably there's a three-year itch! But as the master of your own destiny it is imperative that you keep your business ahead of the game – you should always be evolving.
- We started essentially out of adversity after having been let down by a previous business partner so it is fair to say that there were some blues but it is nearly three years and no itch as things are currently getting better.
- Yes – everyone must do I guess. But the key is to remind yourself why you're doing it and look around. There are plenty of worse options! Seven-month itch is probably more realistic with most I know.

Initial diagnosis

- Remind yourself why you're doing it
- Look around and compare with worse options
- Remember that most people in business have itchy and low times

10–50 staff

- Yes – our third year saw our biggest client stop spending. We had grown every quarter for a year and a half before that and defined much of our business around that client. It led us not only to trade poorly for a while but also to conclude that businesses of our sort could only get 'so big' and that we might be wasting our time. If that hadn't happened we may have broken out from small-to-medium to medium by now, a key step.
- Yes, it can be very frustrating especially if you've come from a larger company to be small and treated as small.
- Multiple itches (normally when things are slow).
- All the time. But that's not a bad thing. You should continually question what your company does and how well it does it. It can be frustrating and uncomfortable if that is difficult to maintain or to communicate, but it is better than risking complacency.
- No. I was advised to give it at least 18 months – after about six I knew I would never want to work for anyone else again.
- No, never. I love this business even more now than I did when I set it up 17 years ago.
- No, just the loneliness of the long distance runner.
- No, seven-year itch, yes … 10 years definitely.
- No – always hungry!
- No! I do need the business to invent challenges for itself periodically – re-branding, relaunching services etc., which keeps the stimulation going.
- No – what does happen is that you come to the end of a honeymoon period and you can lose clients or staff. The secret is to tell yourself in advance that it's going to happen, so you are prepared for the emotional shock when it arrives.
- Never heard of it.
- It can be difficult to motivate yourself if you find that you are facing the same problems over and over again so it is important to get external help such as a good non-exec director who can offer a different perspective and a less emotional response. This can help you to solve the problems that make you feel like you are going round in circles.

Initial diagnosis

- Continually question what your business does and how well it does it
- Many people experience the loneliness of the long distance runner
- Tell yourself in advance that the honeymoon period will end
- Get a good non-exec to offer a different, less emotional perspective

More than 50 staff

- Yes … lasted for five years!
- Yes, don't we all? We wouldn't be human otherwise.
- Yes, everyone does. The excitement of the first year or so is replaced by constant anxieties about the business and inevitably earning less money than your mates working for a big company. The payday seems a very long way off.
- Yes. Part of launching a business is that you don't want to 'drive the car' long term after you have built it! It is better to have the idea, build the car, then employ someone else to drive it for you whilst you go build the next one.
- Yes, naturally. How do you keep the momentum and the freshness? Partners will also experience this, so you need to be aware and act sensitively and professionally.
- Post-launch blues yes. Three-year itch yes.
- No. That's a good thing about growing a business. There's always something new.
- I have never run a start-up, but my observation is that it often happens. This is usually about managing size, direction, the development of the partners as leaders and managers, and so on. I observe that many businesses get to a size of around 70–80 and hit a real inflection point: will they power on through and become an enduring brand, or will they stutter or, worse, retract?

  Personally I think this is a function of:

  - Size: suddenly you can't do everything yourself (as a founder)
  - Leadership: you have to begin to lead and inspire others – it's not enough to be small, new and groovy

- Vision: you have to decide what you are about, what your personal and business objectives are (and more importantly get your partners to agree)
- You're not the new kid on the block any more, so you have to work harder to get your message across (to new clients, existing clients, the media, employees, etc.)
- Reality bites: you have to start to spend time worrying about grown-up issues like staff retention, office management, human resources, a bigger building, your founding client getting their own three-year itch, and so on.

- No. The day you decide there is nothing more you can do to improve your business you should do two things. Firstly, fire anyone who agrees with you and then resign yourself. No three-year itch, but it is stressful working with idiots.
- No! But I didn't appreciate the huge difference in commitment between a senior position in someone else's company against having your own company.
- Not really. But at three years you realize the business will never be 'finished', that new challenges emerge to fit the time available!
- After a few months I wondered if I would ever get my life back, or be able to go on holiday. Every now and then I dream of jacking it all in to be a lumberjack or something completely physical, and with no responsibility for anyone or anything. It passes though, and 98 times out of 100 I'm more than delighted with running my own business. The only thing that has eclipsed it is having a baby. In fact, launching a business is a bit like having a baby. You get the sleepless nights and metaphorical dirty nappies to deal with in the first two years too.

Initial diagnosis

- Have the idea, build the car, then employ someone else to drive it for you
- Realize that the business will never be 'finished'
- Launching a business is a bit like having a baby
- Be aware that partners get the blues too, so act sensitively

Question 3: Did you ever suffer from post-launch blues or a three-year itch?

Overall diagnosis and verdict: Beating the blues

- Regard a launch as the beginning of the beginning rather than the end of the beginning
- Tell yourself in advance that the honeymoon period will end
- Continually question what your business does and how well it does it
- Keep transforming it into a shinier, newer version of itself
- Entrepreneurs are often good 'starters' or 'creators' but poor at routine
- Work out how to deal with the highs and lows
- Give yourself credit for what you have already achieved
- Remind yourself why you're doing it
- Look around and compare with worse options
- You and your partners have to evolve along with your business
- Remember that most people in business have itchy and low times
- Be aware that partners get the blues too, so act sensitively
- Have the idea, build the car, then employ someone else to drive it for you
- Realize that the business will never be 'finished'
- Launching a business is a bit like having a baby
- Running it can be like the loneliness of the long distance runner
- Get a good non-exec to offer a different, less emotional perspective

Question 4: How do you plan the 'next big thing'?

The fourth question deliberately placed the 'next big thing' in inverted commas, to see whether it actually needed to be big or not.

Sole traders

- I think it's important to keep your big picture clear and at the forefront of everything you do. Opportunities will come that require quick decisions that could influence the direction of your growth. For me it's imperative that these are not lost but nor do they set me on a different course from the one on which I started. Basically, be flexible about how you get there but not about where you're going.
- By doing my homework.
- Listen, look, think and make notes.
- Planning for the next big thing is the easy part. The next big thing has to start life as a creative idea. I make sure I'm always tuned into what's happening around me, and set aside time to think outside the box. Usually an idea comes to me when talking to people and hearing about their lives.
- Always scan business press for openings, opportunities and ideas. These leads provide a base for unique initiatives projecting a more customized approach. Being on the receiving end, one thing I hate is a mass-produced mailing for example.
- Next big things insert themselves into my brain continually. I deal with them by talking them through with respected individuals (including clients) who talk me out of them – they know I'm onto a good thing.
- It comes to me. Sometimes figuratively, sometimes literally, like a phone call. If it ever didn't, I'd go for a long walk and then it would.
- I don't think you can – it's like falling in love and you can't plan that. However, there are times in your life when you are likely to be susceptible, and then it's a matter of being very open to new ideas, staying well-informed and making unlikely connections.
- With a lot of careful thought and by talking to people who know more about it than I do.

Initial diagnosis

- Be flexible about how you get there but not about where you're going
- Talk to people and hear about their lives
- Talk to people who know more about it than you do
- Make quick decisions about opportunities that could influence your growth
- Go for a long walk

Small partnerships (two or three people)

- We're not planning the next big thing. In addition to general business and marketing consultancy, we now do headhunting as well as M&A, but neither was planned. We're merely doing what our clients seem to want us to do even if we didn't set out to do either of these. Providing we know what we're doing, enjoy it and make money out of it, that's fine. One of my bosses said to me years ago that there are only three bases for taking on a client:
  1 They'll buy great work from you
  2 You'll have fun
  3 You'll make money.

  Any two will do.
- I don't think you can formally plan for the next big thing. However you must be prepared to chat to many different types of people in different markets and trades to hear lots of ideas and get a feel for possible trends. You then have to be prepared to have a punt on something you feel may succeed even if others don't agree.
- By costing it accurately with realistic financial forecasts, ensuring like-minded people are brought in to support the growth, as we are in a very niche area of our business, and attention to detail really matters, and a company name to live up to.
- You don't. All you can do is be aware of what's going on around you and develop antennae that let you pick up things earlier than everyone else. You only need to be five minutes ahead of the pack to succeed, in fact if you're too far ahead you'll probably fail.

Initial diagnosis

- You only need to be five minutes ahead of the pack to succeed
- Keep your big picture clear and at the forefront of everything you do
- Chat to lots of different types of people in different markets
- There are three bases for taking on a customer: great work, fun and money. Any two will do

Fewer than 10 staff

- Consensually, with the team. I can't deliver this myself.
- My plan is to get us all to plan and for us, that is a big thing – beginning with weekly meetings.
- I have always found that, if you plan the Next Big Thing, it never really works out the way you expect – so I have a somewhat fluid approach to it. I have an idea where I want to go but am always open to other opportunities too. If you are too tunnel vision about where you want to go you can miss out on some other great things.
- With a great deal of luck as well as pluck.
- Just get on with it, keep lifting your head up and be ready to take opportunities.
- By making sure that the company is giving customers what they want, research what else you could offer and plan to add it on to your services.
- Evolution seems to be working for us rather than concentrated planning.
- Sudden inspirations rather than formal planning. Always have a pen and paper handy! Get good thinking time – a good run in the hills usually does it for me. And don't be too disheartened when you inevitably find that someone else has 'done' your idea already.

Initial diagnosis

- Ask your team
- Have an idea where you want to go but always be open to other opportunities
- Don't be too tunnel vision about where you want to go
- Just get on with it
- Keep lifting your head up and be ready to take opportunities
- Get good thinking time: take a good run in the hills
- Always have a pen and paper handy

10–50 staff

- Do the work ourselves. It is easy to be myopic and just get on with business hoping the next thing will just come along. You have to make time for planning, ask people for their input and make your plans. You then have to make sensible budget allocations and back your judgment.

- This depends on what 'the next big thing' is. All innovation should be grounded in the skills base of your company. You should constantly review to ensure that you are doing what you should do properly and see where improvement can be made. That may result in being able to identify an area where you can truly innovate and which will be of interest to your current clients and potential new clients. If the 'next big thing' is thought up and developed in isolation, it is likely that it won't be that big a thing in the long term.
- You don't, it plans you.
- Not strategically enough.
- I don't. My business is the next big thing.
- Talking to bright people. Listening to what is happening around me both politically, economically. Allowing myself the time away from day-to-day pressures to contemplate 'what else'?
- By thinking through where we need to be and then working out the three steps that will get us there.
- Based entirely on market trends, research, studious scrutiny of the competition and educated guess work.
- I am not sure that there is always that much planning. There is always a vision or dream and from somewhere an idea comes that feels spot on.
- It finds you if you are doing the right things.
- Listen to our customers, look how successful businesses managed expansion strategies in other sectors and test it out with lots of people you know before you make a decision.
- Normally very random – on the running machine or in the shower! Very rarely do we sit in a meeting to discuss our next plans formally.
- You have to continue to reinvent your business all the time, as business models become out of date (even if only at the edges) in a frighteningly short space of time. It's the constant planning and executing, planning and executing, that enables you to face fresh challenges. If you wait and deal with the next big thing as a solus event, it becomes a much bigger challenge. It's the same trap as companies having an annual strategy event – strategy is something you should look at regularly, not once a year in an awayday.

Initial diagnosis

- Make time for planning
- Reinvent your business all the time
- Get on the running machine or in the shower
- Listen to your customers and bright people
- Look how successful businesses manage expansion in other sectors
- Test it out with lots of people you know before you make a decision
- Listen to what is happening around you
- Allow yourself the time away to contemplate 'what else?'
- It finds you if you are doing the right things

More than 50 staff

- Be constantly dissatisfied with the status quo. Imagine a place you would love to be in a few years' time that is only just realistic, then plot a route there in three-month increments.
- In terms of new ideas, they just happen through moments of inspiration or opportunistically. I find that if I sit and try and come up with an idea, it doesn't happen. In terms of moving into novel related areas within a business, external consultants and facilitators can help. This is because often it is difficult to see what can be done when you are deep into a business and having a facilitator can focus brainstorming.
- It is better to take a calculated risk than a risk without knowing the consequences.
- Difficult. I think there are two main styles:
  1. Scattergun: some people are just very lateral and very inventive – some of their ideas are inspired, some inevitably not. In this circumstance the business almost becomes an 'energy brand', feeding on the leaders' exciting proposals, and accepting that some will thrive and others not. At the other end of the spectrum:
  2. Institutionalized: the leadership team has to accept and understand that this is an important priority and work (as a team) and in the context of the agreed business vision and objectives towards the generation and execution of 'The Next Big Thing'. I guess this is about blood, sweat, tears and (crucially) making it a priority. I don't know which I prefer.

- Look at what you have and see every permutation to iterate it. Look at the competition. Examine market trends. Then when you are fully appraised read all the papers you can to get ideas, speak with the market and customers. Then think very hard for something innovative – stealing from other industries where appropriate.
- With difficulty as we are risk averse and doing all right without it.
- With difficulty. The day job gets in the way!
- Conversation. Chitchat. Drinks with experts. Fans of your first product telling you what you should do next. Read lots – and read laterally.
- I'm never short of the next big thing – choosing which one is difficult. Priority is key or you can stretch like an elastic band. My ambitions for the company are always way beyond our current reach but that spurs me on. I have these thoughts when I'm away from the business, never when I'm sitting at my desk. You need to get away from the business to have the enlightening moments of inspiration.
- It is essential to have an annual day of reflection – the past, present and future. Doing more of the same is death. Each year have one new initiative, be prepared to try and fail because one will succeed. Keep the business fresh, maintain excitement, and back the people who have ideas.
- Spend some time thinking about it.
- Always start with the people, the casting.

Initial diagnosis

- Start with the people and the casting
- Have an annual day of reflection
- Be spurred on by ambitions that are way beyond your current reach
- Get away from the business to have enlightening moments of inspiration
- Don't sit and try to come up with an idea – it won't happen.
- Use external consultants or facilitators to move into novel related areas

Question 4: How do you plan the 'next big thing'?

Overall diagnosis and verdict: How to plan the Next Big Thing

- Have an idea where you want to go but always be open to other opportunities
- Talk to people who know more about it than you do and hear about their lives
- Make quick decisions about opportunities that could influence your growth
- Go for a long walk, or a run, get on the running machine, or in the shower
- You only need to be five minutes ahead of the pack to succeed
- Keep your big picture clear and at the forefront of everything you do
- Ask your team
- Keep lifting your head up and be ready to take opportunities
- Always have a pen and paper handy
- Make time for planning
- Reinvent your business all the time
- Listen to your customers and bright people
- Look how successful businesses manage expansion in other sectors
- Listen to what is happening around you
- Allow yourself the time away to contemplate 'what else?'
- Start with the people and the casting
- Have an annual day of reflection
- Be spurred on by ambitions that are way beyond your current reach
- Get away from the business to have enlightening moments of inspiration
- Use external consultants or facilitators to move into novel related areas

Question 5: If you could have known one thing when you started that you know now, what would it be?

Question five attempts to reveal what people have learnt over the years, and help the reader avoid repeating mistakes already made by others.

Sole traders

- Networking is essential as talent alone in some cases is not enough.
- A clearer picture of my worth in the marketplace.
- To know which 50 per cent of the clichés about starting businesses were true.
- It's tough as hell but worth the struggle.
- Listen to your gut feeling, as it's usually right.
- A greater understanding of the selling points which best trigger an income generating response. And being more confident about it.
- Difficult, very difficult, to answer. I would like to say that I wish I'd known how long it was going to take to get it off the ground (two years). However, had I known that and articulated it to those who have supported me, I might not have done it. Catch 22.
- No one's as surprised by your fees as you are – but repeat business still has its price-elasticity limits. Staying gung-ho on price is one way to appear good at what you do, but it doesn't work like that in all disciplines. People often perceive they can buy what you sell from a cheaper source. The trick is keeping them reminded of why you're worth it.
- Equity is forever. Be very careful about who you cut in on an equity basis as it will be very hard or expensive to extricate them further down the track. Profit share generally achieves a lot of the same incentivization, particularly when your shares aren't publicly traded.
- Working on your own can be a lonesome business. This is compounded by the attitude of many others (who don't work for themselves) who often view the self-employed as being semi-retired people working only when they feel like it. Being your own boss does allow you to be flexible, but in my experience it can also often mean working harder because no

one else will do it for you and if you don't do it, you don't get paid.

- That two years later I'd be back in employment again.

Initial diagnosis

- Equity is forever. Be very careful to whom you give equity
- Networking is essential as talent alone in some cases is not enough
- Have a clear picture of your worth in the marketplace
- Understand the selling points which trigger income-generating responses
- Listen to your gut feeling – it's usually right
- Be confident
- Be aware that it takes longer to launch a business than anyone ever thinks
- If *you* don't do it, you don't get paid

Small partnerships (two or three people)

- If you get into business with other people in any kind of shared ownership be crystal clear on who you think your clients are, what you think your service or product is and what it does for your customers, how that is going to be delivered and by whom, and exactly what each of you bring to, and take out of, the business.
- I sort of knew it. And wasn't wrong. Things never happen as quickly as you want and need.
- That potential clients lie, and however ethically you may run your business the waters are still shark infested. Cynical and naive at the same time maybe, but a tough lesson to learn.
- Taking the pressure off by realizing that you've got enough cash in the bank to feed your family for a year because it's really not going to be all that simple!
- If we knew what we know now before we started we would have done it earlier! The business has evolved relatively smoothly and new business has come our way as our reputation has grown, which has been rewarding. We have never really had to pitch hard for new accounts. Conversely, until quite recently we have never considered growing the business and actively seeking more lucrative accounts.

- All businesses are people businesses. Invest in friendships and relationships and the rest will happen quite naturally.

Initial diagnosis

- All businesses are people businesses
- Invest in friendships and relationships – the rest will happen naturally
- Things never happen as quickly as you want or need

Fewer than 10 staff

- Firstly how tough it can be sometimes, and secondly that it is the same for everyone else in business. It's easy to get down when things don't go as planned and easy to take it personally when it is your own business. I wish I had been told that everyone running and growing a business goes through some big lows. That is when you need to keep motivated and positive and keep going.
- However hard you think it is to take the plunge, it's only the beginning and there's a whole lot more hardship to follow. That's not to say it's not fun, just make sure you're prepared for the rollercoaster ride you're going to take, and recognize that there's no longer a choice between 'work to live' or 'live to work' as the divide between personal life and work to all intents disappears.
- Get a good bookkeeper and chase those invoices!
- Competitors are just that. They will kill for your business.
- To keep cool and remember that running your own business is, and will always be, a rollercoaster ride, try to enjoy the ups and not get too uptight about the downs.
- That not everyone will be as committed as you are. Keep your shareholding lean and mean.
- To be more ambitious from day one. Have a medium-term plan and go for it, not deal in the short-term issues.
- Given the time in my life of starting the current business, I think it would be better if I had known less rather than more.
- The total and all-consuming nature of your own thing. And all the needless paperwork!

Initial diagnosis

- Everyone running a business goes through some big lows
- Make sure you're prepared for the rollercoaster ride
- Not everyone will be as committed as you are

10–50 staff

- It takes a lot longer than you think.
- You have to invest to reap returns (not just hard work).
- The importance of doing new business work when the business is flourishing rather than waiting until you need it. The importance of your existing business in a growth strategy.
- One thing? Gosh, there's so much. Probably I'd have honed my financial skills. You need to see at a glance the comings and goings of your money.
- EVERYTHING is negotiable.
- The real costs of doing business – all the hidden extras around employing people.
- Work on your business not in it. The three ways to grow your business (more punters, increased frequency and increased value of sale).
- I think it is that once you run your own business you will never switch off. You will be constantly thinking about it. This doesn't matter as long as you are enjoying your job but it is a mistake to start a business thinking it will give you a better work–life balance than working for someone else. You can sometimes spend less time in the office but you will spend a lot more time thinking about work.
- Be braver and trust your instincts.
- If you think you have reached the right decision don't hesitate. Your first instincts are normally right.
- Business is not personal. It's business, so treat it that way! Bitterness is not in the dictionary of the entrepreneur. If it is, then see section entitled: 'Waste of time: being bitter.'
- That the audience we are selling to know less about our subject matter than we do. We always felt like the new boys and our confidence suffered as a consequence. If we had known this from the start our growth would have been quicker.

- Get the business plan or structure right, at the outset. Once you have started, it's too late to go back and change things. So plan, plan, plan; test, test, test, before you set up.
- You have much more space to be radical in how you run your company than you think. There is a tendency to try to fit your service and offer around the people and the assets that you have, rather than examine how best to do what you are best at.
- Getting established in a proper office of your own does wonders for the confidence.

Initial diagnosis

- It takes a lot longer than you think
- Plan and test everything before you set up
- Your customers know less about your subject matter than you do
- Business is not personal
- If you think you have reached the right decision don't hesitate
- Your first instincts are normally right
- Everything is negotiable

More than 50 staff

- Know who to trust, work with complimentary talent, and always act and tell the truth fast.
- Business is fundamentally simple: revenue minus costs equals profit.
- Not to keep pursuing something that you have built if it isn't a success.
- Some things you do work, some don't. If you have a dead horse on your hands, don't waste time flogging it forever. Set yourself a limit as to how much time you will put in to your 'Problem Child' and, once that limit is reached, drop it and move on to the next thing.
- The job never feels done (because it never is).
- Good things come to those that wait and most new business is never more than a learning curve.
- Few other people are as excited by your business as you are.
- That a business comprising five equal partners can be a curse as well as a blessing. That clear roles – if not hierarchies – must be established.

- That you can't be good at everything and if you can't add up and you're a bit short on organizational skills and process, get a person who is to do your finances and chase in the money. Likewise if you like writing the invoices and counting the money, get someone in who can sell like hell. Play to your personal strengths and surround yourself with people who more than make up for your weaknesses.
- Whilst we did have excellent financial management, the one thing that I underestimated was the critical importance of matching growth with cash flow management. Cash is king, profit is clearly essential but when the profit is generated, it may not match the needs of the business in terms of surplus cash. I found the banks utterly useless in supporting a rapidly growing business. They were inflexible, they always turned a drama into a crisis, and they seemed to get more anxious the more successful the business became. So my mantra would be: cash is king, never be caught short.
- It is always about people, people, people.
- Talented craftsmen are by no means talented managers.

Initial diagnosis

- It is always about people, people, people
- Always act and tell the truth fast
- Talented craftsman are by no means talented managers
- Cash is king – never be caught short
- Few other people are as excited by your business as you are
- Don't keep pursuing something if it isn't a success

Question 5: If you could have known one thing when you started that you know now, what would it be?

Overall diagnosis and verdict: If I'd known this when I started ...

- Plan and test everything before you set up
- Be confident and have a clear picture of your worth
- Equity is forever. Be very careful to whom you give equity
- Everything takes a lot longer than you think

- Make sure you're prepared for the rollercoaster ride
- Networking is essential as talent alone in some cases is not enough
- Invest in friendships and relationships – the rest will happen naturally
- Understand the selling points which trigger income-generating responses
- Listen to your gut feeling – it's usually right
- All businesses are people businesses
- Everyone running a business goes through some big lows
- Few other people are as excited by your business or as committed as you are
- Your customers know less about your subject matter than you do
- Business is not personal
- Your first instincts are normally right
- Everything is negotiable
- It is always about people, people, people
- Always act and tell the truth fast
- Talented craftsmen are by no means talented managers
- Don't keep pursuing something if it isn't a success
- If *you* don't do it, you don't get paid

Question 6: Is there anything else you would like to pass on about growing or evolving your business?

The last question is totally open-ended, allowing people to pass on any helpful knowledge that could serve the reader well.

Sole traders

- I'm still a minnow; ask me when I'm a pike.
- If you really believe in yourself, and in what you want to achieve, you owe it to yourself to give it a go, regardless of any negative outside opinion.
- Stick with it – starting a business is like batting like Boycott (boring, unglamorous, yet remarkably rewarding for brute perseverance).
- You have to love what you do. Let me say that again: YOU HAVE TO LOVE WHAT YOU DO. Basically, everyone is selling something, and if you can't get excited about what

you're selling, how will the client? Be patient and be ready to act when the right opportunities or ideas present themselves. Always have a forward plan to work to. Writing forward plans and lists is time well spent. Within growing any business, people skills are paramount. Develop 100 per cent faith and persistence.

- Take all reasonable steps to prevent business leaving but do not get hung up on it. If it wants to go, let it go and remember it fondly. The important thing is to keep it coming in through the front door.
- Setting deadlines is good. Hunger is useful. Greed is usually transparent. You're probably better than you think you are. There are some people it's just not worth trying with.
- Never underestimate the value of talking to people about it. Anyone, everyone. And make sure you enjoy the process of building the business, not just the dream of what you will one day achieve.

Initial diagnosis

- You have to love what you do
- Write forward plans and lists
- Greed is usually transparent
- You're probably better than you think you are
- There are some people it's just not worth trying with
- Enjoy the process of building the business, not just the dream of what you will one day achieve

Small partnerships (two or three people)

- You can't possibly know everything. Talk to as many people as possible in the same or different industries and also to people with varied experience.
- Business is not a science but an art. You need to be able to adapt to different situations; a combination of yours and other people's experience will help you do that well.
- Yes. When you make a phone call, write a letter, attend a meeting or make a new business presentation, there are only three possible outcomes. The customer, potential or current, is either going to like it, loathe it, or be undecided. None of these are personal, so be brave, say what you really think, and go to bed knowing you did your best.

- We started as a partnership six-and-a-half years ago (and later became a limited company) and after three years employed one part-time assistant who is now full time. To be honest at the outset it was never about making serious money but has given us – the two directors – a comfortable income. The position we are in now is that one or other of us may want to step aside in a few years and at this stage the company is not 'worth anything' unless we grow it. We have come to realize that we'd like some reward at the end of, say, ten years. We would need to employ account managers that our clients are totally comfortable with. Currently the company is simply the reputation of the two of us in the trade. And the travel industry is renowned for low, low margins and expectations are high for very low returns. We are trying to change this image and provide better services to show that higher fees are justified and in the long run make sense. So for others setting up or growing, don't sell yourselves too cheap, don't be afraid to move on from something if it is not working – we have resigned accounts but never lost one and if we feel uncomfortable with someone or with falling standards, we move on.
- Businesses evolve, and the best ones are rarely the same now as when they started out – so embrace change and accept that the important thing is to stay in business and grow. The rest is secondary.
- Nah. Go make the mistakes and learn.

Initial diagnosis

- Be brave, say what you really think, and go to bed knowing you did your best
- Make mistakes and learn
- Don't sell yourself too cheap
- Don't be afraid to move on from something if it is not working

Fewer than 10 staff

- At some stage in your life, go for your own business – it may not suit you and you may end up back in the corporate world, but equally you may find that you love being master of your own destiny – and it would be a hell of a shame to look back one day and regret that you'd never tested your mettle.

- Make sure you like what you are doing and be with the people you enjoy being with.
- Reputation in any market is worth more than anything else.
- Your family is more important than anything else. Don't exclude them from what's going on, you'll need them for the ups as well as the downs.
- Get the team around you right.
- It's not easy!
- Have fun with the people that you are in business with.
- Don't be afraid to make mistakes. Just don't make the same mistake again and learn from the experience. Be willing to listen to customers and be quick to adapt your product or service – no one is loyal these days.

Initial diagnosis

- Make sure you like what you are doing and be with the people you enjoy being with
- Reputation in any market is worth more than anything else

10–50 staff

- Get a good lawyer and accountant and don't believe that banks are there to help.
- Talk things through with friends, peers, colleagues, and even rivals. It is amazing how many people have a genuine and unselfish interest in your business and also what interesting pieces of insight and advice that they are prepared to share.
- Build a company that is right for you, not what you think companies are meant to be like. If you only want to work two days a week, then build a company around that.
- Listen to your clients, keep your business proposition simple and hire hungry, enthusiastic people to deliver it and reward them when they do.
- Work out what you are good or great at and try to sell that hard rather than just trying to sell what you think the market wants today, as customers will see through you when you are selling things you aren't good at and you will have less business in the area in which you do excel.
- Believe in what you are doing and at the same time listen to healthy criticism. Surround yourself with people who are as passionate as you and have skills where you know you have

weaknesses. Business is more than making money. It is in fact rather like a child growing up, so accept that there will be teething problems, and that it will face adolescent tantrums. It also needs to have an honest soul so treat all people as you would expect to be treated yourself. What you put in is largely what you get out. Take time out, because your business will be there when you get back and you will see more clearly what you are doing right as well as wrong, with the proper balance in your life.

- My responses:
  - If you want it badly enough anything is possible.
  - Business is about making sales and cash flow. If you keep an eye on those two, everything else can be managed.
  - Prioritize – do the important things first, don't put them off.
  - Client service – most businesses (in the UK) are so bad at it that being better than the competition is easy to do and gives you a huge advantage.
- Be absolutely committed to what you do – this is MUCH more than just being interested. Successful businesses are the ones that add greater value than their competitors. Strive to build the strongest possible rapport between you and your customers. Know the difference between a sale and a customer. Never, ever forget the importance of after sales. Never, ever ignore your competition. Never, ever think you're safe. Absolutely every cliché about cash being king is right. Do EVERYTHING you can to let cash flow into your business. Take no prisoners with credit control! You CAN be too busy!
- Don't waste money on anything.
- Never be afraid to ask advice from someone you admire.
- Watch the figures like a hawk and believe them. Seek guidance from an independent business consultant or Managing Director.
- Just because you have been successful in the past doesn't mean you are going to be successful in the future. Never be complacent, always seek to improve, innovate and re-invent your offer.
- My golden rules if I did it again:
  - Select the right business advisers from the start – don't just phone the first you see in *Yellow Pages*!
  - Tie key staff in with incentives and be generous, but identify those that are key and those that are not.

  - Be absolutely clear about what your product or service is and focus, focus, focus – this will ensure your clients (and your internal team) have a total understanding about the business's reason for being.
  - Create a distinct business culture – it will reward you in the long run with loyal, motivated staff.
  - Decide how you are going to maintain the same service levels as you grow and you are relying on others to deliver them.
  - Make sure your financial reporting systems and team are strong before you deliver an aggressive growth plan.
  - Cash and funding are critical – be pessimistic.
  - Keep a close eye on overheads in the early years.
- Get the business plan or structure right, at the outset. Once you have started, it's too late to go back and change things. So plan, plan, plan; test, test, test, before you set up.
- I'm pleased to say our company is doing well at the moment. I think we are doing better than our peers who started up in business at about the same time as us. Thinking about why we are flourishing and they seem not to be, it struck me that we appointed a non-executive Chairman at the outset (he was very much part of our planning since inception, actually). He has proved to be a potent 'secret weapon', as his experience is invaluable and he has the ability to defuse matters which, if left unchecked, could escalate to threaten relationships amongst the other shareholders. Anyone setting up in business should give serious thought to acquiring such a Chairman.

Initial diagnosis

- Never be afraid to ask advice from someone you admire
- Do the important things first – don't put them off
- Treat all people as you would expect to be treated yourself
- Believe in what you are doing and at the same time listen to healthy criticism
- Select the right business advisors from the start
- Be absolutely clear about what your product or service is
- Past success doesn't mean future success

More than 50 staff

- Keep the management team small and only have people on the Board or in the management team who are good at managing. There is a temptation to reward by giving directorships to people who have performed really well in the tasks they do, but they may not necessarily have the qualities to manage a business. Additionally, they may not actually want to take on, or be aware of, the fiduciary responsibilities that come with being a director. Business evolution over the years has dictated this myth that to be a success you ultimately become a director. This is, however, wrong. Reward people for excellent performance and make them champions in their own right, but only have a management team consisting of those that can manage.
- Be smart, do the proper due diligence, listen to the market. Do not over invest, be clear and focused in your proposition. Work with clients and people you like and respect.
- You need a very good management team to succeed.
- Beware of the cost of sale – the up-front investment has to be commensurate with the reward for success.
- You have to enjoy it!!
- Keep clients happy. They are your best new business tool (more work from them, more work from them telling others how great you are).
- My advice to anyone considering their business future would be to have Big Audacious Goals. A 10 per cent growth in income each year is fine but not exactly exciting. I have been fortunate to work with people who have crazy goals and it's funny how they seem to do very well compared with the people who plod along. Apologies to Leo Burnett because I'll get this wrong but he said something like, 'If you reach for the stars you might not quite get there but you won't come up with a handful of mud either'. Too right.
- Never talk about it as 'your' business. Everyone who works for you or who has worked for you has had a role in the success of your business. Recognize and reward them for that – verbally if not financially. The person who thinks they did it all by themselves will be either a very lonely person or will have a revolving door of people coming and going. Let everyone feel it's their business and let everyone have a clear role in the development and progression of the business – but never let more than 50 per cent of the shares go if you want to stay in control.

- Be serious from the outset about your customer data, what you know about them, and also about your own internal knowledge. It might be boring at the start but just wait until you have hundreds or thousands of customers and you realize that you haven't got the systems in place to tell you anything meaningful about them. Marketing meets technology meets knowledge management … that's the basis of a great business in the future.
- Don't hesitate to give it a go as long as you have a clear sense of purpose and at least one partner.

Initial diagnosis

- If you reach for the stars you might not quite get there but you won't come up with a handful of mud either.

Question 6: Is there anything else you would like to pass on about growing or evolving your business?

Overall diagnosis and verdict: Pass it on

- You have to love what you do
- Be absolutely clear about what your product or service is
- Greed is usually transparent
- You're probably better than you think you are – don't sell yourself too cheap
- There are some people it's just not worth trying with
- Enjoy the process of building the business, not just the dream of what you will one day achieve
- Be brave, say what you really think, and go to bed knowing you did your best
- Make mistakes and learn
- Don't be afraid to move on from something if it is not working
- Be with the people you enjoy being with
- Reputation in any market is worth more than anything else
- Never be afraid to ask advice from someone you admire
- Do the important things first – don't put them off
- Treat all people as you would expect to be treated yourself

- Believe in what you are doing and at the same time listen to healthy criticism
- Past success doesn't mean future success
- Reach for the stars

Chapter 6 recap: whole survey diagnosis

I appreciate that this was not so much a chapter as a set of survey findings. I thought long and hard about adding too much analysis to the comments, and resisted the temptation because they very much speak for themselves. The collected work is a veritable powerhouse of business thought, and I have pulled it all together in the appendix as 110 pieces of other people's wisdom. Of course, there are some contradictory comments, but a theme running through it all is the value of paying attention to the experiences of others, and to experts such as non-executive directors and outside advisers who are less emotionally attached to the business. Beware the casual advisor or the quick fix, don't cut corners and arrive in the wrong place, and bear in mind cheap advice can often be the most expensive.

One other theme I think is worth commenting on. Although I have stressed that this is not a quantitative survey, it looks very much to me as though growth becomes much more important the larger your company gets. In the main, sole traders, partnerships and companies with fewer than ten staff are very apprehensive about growth. Those with several hundred employees think it is pretty much essential to retain momentum, or to placate shareholders. This is not statistically verifiable, but the sway of opinion is that anxieties about growth are more acute the more people you have – something of an irony.

With regard to the evolutive thinking method, you have nearly finished stage three. Stage one gathered the facts, stage two added your own opinion, and now you have seen the opinions of others. There is only one remaining question you need to ask yourself about what you have read in this chapter:

- What can I learn from what other people have been through?

Take your list of ideas and consider them in the context of all the advice here. If anything has touched a particular nerve in relation to your business, then have a think and make the necessary changes.

You have now completed the evolutive thinking process, and also the Hone phase of the CHEW system. In phase III, Evolve, we will engineer some personal and organizational ways in which to make it all happen.

Cautionary Tale: Barry Brown, the accountant who re-built the straitjackets he left his previous company to avoid

Barry worked for one of the big four accountancy firms, and rose steadily to the top of the pile, although, as we all know, it's hard to prove that you are in charge of anything in an accountancy firm. As the years rolled by, he became more and more frustrated with the bureaucracy and systems, and he eventually concluded that there must be a better way.

He resigned and set up his own accountancy firm. This was not going to be a one-man band, but a pocket battleship that could be far more adventurous and flexible than the lumbering behemoth he had left behind. He started with all the zeal of a start-up, picked up good early business, and enjoyed the freedom of doing his own thing making his own decisions.

Soon he had 30 staff, and as time went on they would ask more and more what the system was for a certain aspect of the business. There were none as such, so reluctantly he accepted that they needed some. He didn't find this part of the business particularly interesting, so when it came to finances, human resources, workflow, recruitment and the other hygiene stuff, he simply copied how it was done in his previous company.

Three years later the business had 55 staff, and Barry was surprised to be confronted by one of them over a drink one day complaining that the company was bureaucratic, and that the systems were stifling rapid and lively business practice. The complainant even went so far as to suggest that clients had pointed it out too.

Barry was vexed. How had it come to this? It was only then that he realized that his lack of attention to putting the right systems in place meant that he had unwittingly replicated the conditions of his former firm. He felt they were straitjackets then, and now he had simply copied them, and brought all their faults along with him. He should have paid more attention in the first place, even if it wasn't his favourite subject.

In this phase you will learn:

- how to change your behaviour to get things done
- how to set up your business tripwires
- how to get comfortable with yourself

The Evolve phase is shorter because you have broken the back of it by now and done the majority of the hard work. This is where we move from discussion of broad concepts to being a bit more prescriptive about what you have to do. It shows you how to distil, articulate and write down what you want for your business and, critically, for yourself. If you do the one without the other, you have only done half the job. In other words, there is no point in 'fixing' the business if you haven't taken the time to think about yourself.

The business element involves setting up tripwires that force the right things to happen, whether you find it easy or not. That means arranging things in advance so that you have less hassle, and less stress, over the coming year. If that doesn't force you into action, detonating some grenades might (read on!). The personal part involves writing your own Lifesmile Statement. This has elements of lifestyle built into it, naturally, but the most important part is working out what really makes you happy. You will be forced to think about it, write it down and, once you have taken the trouble to do that, it tends to occur. The knack with this phase is to write down exactly what you want, and when you want it. That makes it much more likely to happen.

set up your business tripwires and grenades

In this chapter you will learn:

- **how to trip yourself up on purpose**
- **how to set up idea, personal and business tripwires**
- **how to detonate idea, personal and business grenades**
- **the value of rapid sequential tasking**
- **how to put the effort in only where it gets you somewhere**

How to trip yourself up on purpose

So you have done a lot of thinking, and now is the time to decide how precisely you are going to implement the great ideas you have generated. We don't want them languishing on a piece of paper in a drawer somewhere and never seeing the light of day. Getting them done will require a mixture of business effort and personal effort, and in this chapter we are going to deal with the business perspective. It is all about setting up your business tripwires so that you cannot fail to action something. Many of us know that if we don't write something down, we will most likely forget it. That could be a sticky note on the back of the door saying 'don't forget keys', a shopping list, or a note on the steering wheel saying 'oil' or 'petrol'. Whatever the task, if you write it down and put it in the right place, it becomes impossible to forget the important thing when the time comes. This is the principle behind business tripwires. We are going to work out what will go wrong *before* it does, and put the measures in place to prevent that from happening. To make this really effective, you need to have the drains up and work out how everything works, and work out where it is most likely to fall down. Predict that, and you will ensure that the important things truly get done.

> **'If you're going to do something, go start. Life's simpler than we sometimes can admit.'** *Robert De Niro*

Write it down and it gets done

Discussing broad concepts in their embryonic phase can be fun, particularly for those who don't have to get the thing in question done. But nothing irritates a decent business person more than a good idea that hasn't quite seen the light of day. No one cares why – the point is, it is still on the drawing board and the fruits of it have not been realized. Often this is because there is confusion about whose responsibility it actually is. Other times it is because the idea is allowed to drift and no one pushes for any particular deadline to be met. The trick is to write it down. As Robert De Niro says, if you intend to start, then start. It's that simple. The precise list of what needs to be done will depend on which ideas you have come up with and what matters most to your business, but we will start with some likely subjects, and you can customize the system to reflect your own circumstances. Here are some examples of idea tripwires.

Idea tripwires

- How is this idea going to get done?
- Who is going to do it?
- By when?

Repeat this process for every idea. If the answer to any question is longer than one word, be suspicious of it. If it is longer than a sentence, it won't get done, so try again. If the answer to the second question is you, then write reminders in your personal organizer now to make sure it gets done. If the answer is someone other than you, get them to agree that they will, and put the same tripwires in their organizer. The date by which it gets done needs careful thought. If you can trust yourself to meet a deadline, then great. If you can't, then put the necessary reminders in the way before it becomes time critical, and set yourself sanctions for missing your own timings. Don't fudge this. In his book *Simply Brilliant,* Fergus O'Connell points out that things either are or they aren't. In other words, they are either done or not done. So don't console yourself with unhelpful thoughts such as 'I'm halfway through it' or 'It's all in hand'. It is either finished, and ready to go public, or it isn't, and if it isn't, it's either late or useless. If you want to know more about this clear way of thinking, there is a summary of the book in the appendix.

> **'To undertake is to achieve.'** *Emily Dickinson*

Now set up your tripwires by getting up close and personal. Answer these questions and, crucially, enact right now the thing that will make sure it happens.

Personal planning tripwires

- What will make me get this done?
- Is that bulletproof, or too flimsy?
- Does that allow me to wriggle out of it later?
- If so, what sanction will force me to do it?
- Have I actually put that in place right now?

There is no room for excuses here because it is completely in your interests to get the thing done, even if it does lie a little way in the future. This technique works for specific items, but it also works for the overall shape of your business. If that is an exercise that you would find useful, then you might want to write down your one-year, three-year, five-year and ten-year aims. Actually, the time spans don't matter, but the principle does. Choose frequencies that are appropriate to your business, and write down the answers to these questions.

Business planning tripwires

- What, ultimately, do I want for my business?
- By when?
- How exactly am I going to get there?
- Do I need help, and if so, from whom?
- Have I started yet?

'The beginning is half of every action.' *Greek proverb*

Whoever the Greek person was, they had it right. The world is full of people who claim to have lots of ideas but, strangely, haven't quite started them. Do not allow yourself to be one of these people. Get started immediately, and learn as you go. You can always change your plan on the way, but don't fall into the trap of standing around pontificating when you could be using the time to get the thing done.

Dropping grenades in fishponds

There is another technique that works for some people who need constant reminders to get organized and get stuff done. I call it dropping grenades in fishponds. The idea here is that you deliberately create cataclysmic circumstances in order to jolt yourself into doing the necessary thing. Some people need a severe shock to force them to do something, so here is a form of disaster planning that may help catapult you into action. We will call them grenades.

Cataclysm (noun): violent upheaval

Idea tripwires

- How is this idea going to get done?
- Who is going to do it?
- By when?

Personal planning tripwires

- What will make me get this done?
- Is that bulletproof, or too flimsy?
- Does that allow me to wriggle out of it later?
- If so, what sanction will force me to do it?
- Have I actually put that in place right now?

Business planning tripwires

- What, ultimately, do I want for my business?
- By when?
- How exactly am I going to get there?
- Do I need help, and if so, from whom?
- Have I started yet?

figure 5 tripwires checklist

The purpose of these questions is not to scare you senseless and prevent you from sleeping well. It is to scare up the important issues for those who bumble along for too long without actually getting done the bits that they know in their hearts will really make a difference.

Idea grenades

- What if this were the only idea available?
- What if it never happened?
- What if there were 20 more like this?

You can see how this extreme line of questioning pushes everything that bit further. Go a bit over the top to test your mettle. If this were the only idea you had, would you still do it? There's no point in wasting time on tripwires and implementation if you aren't convinced, and if you aren't, then why should your colleagues or customers be?

Personal grenades

- What if I could never work again?
- What if I took a year off?
- What if I quit this and did something totally different?

These are pretty poignant too, and the intention is to make you stop and think so that you can work out the severity of an item and how badly you want to do it. Then, if you conclude that it definitely does matter, you can engineer the necessary tripwires. We will investigate all this further in the next chapter when you write your Lifesmile Statement.

Business grenades

- What if the business folded tomorrow?
- What if all the staff were fired?
- What if all our customers suddenly disappeared?

Nasty scorched earth scenarios like this are very polarizing and are good for helping you to clarify your thoughts so that you really know what you are trying to achieve. The principle is the same as for your personal issues. Use this Armageddon approach to determine how badly something matters, and how you are going to guarantee that it gets done.

Idea grenades

- What if this were the only idea available?
- What if it never happened?
- What if there were twenty more like this?

Personal grenades

- What if I could never work again?
- What if I took a year off?
- What if I quit this and did something totally different?

Business grenades

- What if the business folded tomorrow?
- What if all the staff were fired?
- What if all our cutomers suddenly disappeared?

figure 6 grenades checklist

Don't replace the original, replace the spare

We are working on the principle here that small reminders yield big results. It just depends how severe a memory jog you require, and only you can be the judge of that. If you are quite efficient, then you may not need any of these measures at all. If you have trouble with motivation, or you are a bit disorganized, then you may well do. Put the appropriate number of tripwires in place, but don't overdo it to the point that they are constantly preventing you from doing the task in hand. They are there to make you do things, not to stop you from doing them. If you put too many in place, you will be damming up the river to see how it flows, which would be pointless. Or, put another way, pulling the flowers up to see how they grow.

But there are also simple principles you can apply that save prevarication in your working day, week or year. One of my favourites is don't replace the original, replace the spare. Every good chef knows that you need a spare of everything, so that when you run out of the original, you simply reach for it, and the meal still happens. Many people in life never have a spare, so whenever they run out of something there is a panic. They then either rush about in a mad flap to buy another item, thus increasing their stress, or the meal doesn't happen. The analogy applies equally to those in business. Whether it is supplies or human resource, you always need a spare. When the spare is used up, buy another spare. Don't replace the original, replace the spare.

Multitasking versus Rapid Sequential Tasking

Part of the knack of making sure things get done is realizing what you are actually capable of doing. Getting a lot done is often associated with multitasking, and there has been a lot of discussion recently about whether everyone is able to do it.

Multitask (verb): to work at several different tasks simultaneously

One theory suggests that women are far better at multitasking than men, and the evidence for that looks quite convincing. So if you are male and no good at multitasking, what can you do? My suggestion is Rapid Sequential Tasking. If you can only do one thing at a time, then do it fast and move on to the next thing. Everyone has checklists, and they usually contain a curious mixture of important and trivial things to do. My research in scores of training sessions suggests that the average number of items on a checklist is between seven and twenty. If it is less than seven, there is no need for a list, and if it is longer than twenty, then the list is too demoralizing so the small things aren't added to it. So strip out the easy trivia from the important stuff, and rattle through it sequentially and quickly. Just because guys apparently can't 'do' multitasking, it doesn't mean they can't do Rapid Sequential Tasking.

Put the effort in only where it gets you somewhere

Your ability to get stuff done is one thing. Whether you are doing the *right* stuff in the first place is a completely different matter. Any good business person will tell you that you need to develop the knack of working out whether you are pursuing the right opportunities, and deciding how much time and effort to spend on them. One of the hardest decisions to make is to pull out of something when you have invested a lot of physical and emotional energy into it. But pull out is precisely what you must do if the thing in question is going nowhere. This was a recurring theme in chapter 6.

> **'If at first you don't succeed, try, try again. Then give up. No use being a damn fool about it.'** *W. C. Fields*

Try again by all means, and again. But don't keep repeating the same mistakes or misjudgements. In my previous book, I offered the following quote in the context of staying sane when running your own business. It has resonated with many since then, but for a slightly different reason than that which I intended at the time.

> **'The definition of insanity is doing the same thing over and over again and expecting different results.'** *Benjamin Franklin*

At the time, I was contrasting this state of affairs with that of being sane, but here we are discussing what level of tenacity is required to get something done, and what judgement is required to decide when to retire gracefully. W. C. Fields suggests a fair bit of tenacity, coupled with the good sense to give up eventually when you have got nowhere.

> **'If at first you don't succeed, try, try again. Then use a stunt double.'** *Arnold Schwarzenegger*

Alternatively, you might conclude that you can't do something, but someone else can. There's nothing wrong with that, and chapter 6 revealed scores of examples of people who strongly recommended complementing your own skills with those of outsiders and partners to make sure the job gets done.

That completes the setting up of your business tripwires, and possibly the detonation of some grenades. Now that you have worked out precisely what you want from your business, in the next chapter we will move on to identifying what you want from your personal life.

Chapter 7 recap

1. How have you arranged to trip yourself up?
2. Over what time period?
3. Have you put it in your personal organizer?
4. Have you written it all down?
5. What sanctions have you imposed on yourself?
6. Have you resolved your idea, personal and business tripwires?
7. Have you detonated your idea, personal and business grenades?
8. Have you remembered to replace the spare, not the original?
9. Are you a multitasker or a Rapid Sequential Tasker?
10. Are you flogging any dead horses?

Success Story: Richard Harrison, the information services Chief Executive who reinvented himself in pharmaceuticals

Sometimes you just have to sit back and admit that what you are currently doing isn't what you want. For some it happens at university when they begin a law degree and then move to modern languages. For others, it happens after they have experienced a first taste of working life in a traineeship. Worst of all, it happens when you are in your mid-30s, when you have responsibilities and have grown used to a substantial income.

That's when you have to reinvent yourself, and that's precisely what Richard did. After rising to the top in a large information services business, he became thoroughly bored and began to question whether he should be in the industry at all. He eventually decided to leave, but not before he had a cunning plan.

Actually, it wasn't that cunning. It would involve a heavy investment of cash, a lot of support from his partner and a large leap of faith. He would fund himself through business school and emerge equipped to run another type of business. He didn't know at this stage what type, and this was an uncertain element of his plan, but he knew he had to adapt to be happy in whatever work he chose to earn a living.

He discussed it with his wife, spoke to the bank, and rustled all his savings together. It was two years of hell. The work was hard and all consuming. It put a strain on his finances and his relationship. But he ploughed on through, completed the exams and passed. He had arrived on the other side – now what?

Throughout his study time, he had been on the lookout for a new potential field of business that he would enjoy, and he found one that took his fancy – pharmaceutical distribution. He had always been interested in healthcare delivery, and the privatization of many aspects of it had allowed him to design a business model that might work. He even made it the subject of his thesis.

Five years later, Richard had realized his ambition, and all because he had the bravery to reinvent himself.

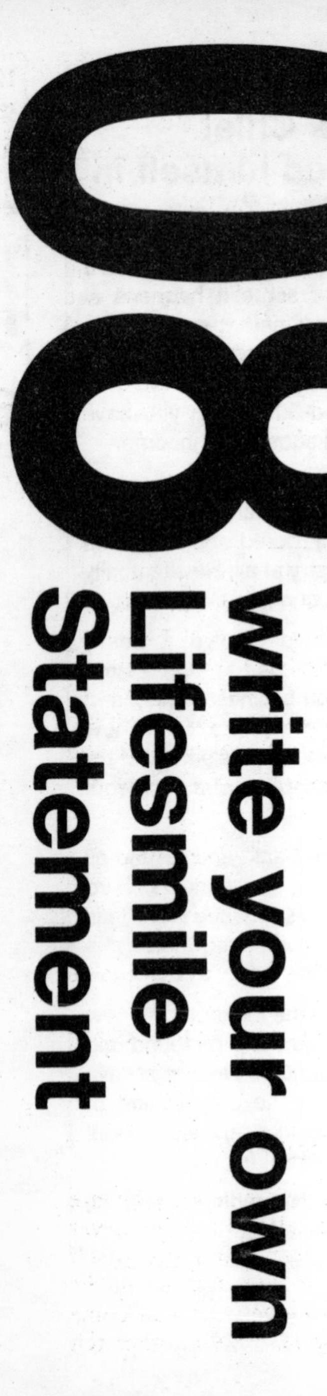

08 write your own Lifesmile Statement

In this chapter you will learn:

- **how to work out what you are like**
- **how to decide your own style**
- **how to decide what you *really* want**
- **how to write your own lifesmile statement**
- **how to have a board meeting with yourself**

Just a quick reminder of where we are in the CHEW system, for those of you who are working your way rigorously through it. C was for Confront, so we have faced up to the hard stuff. H was for Hone, where we developed ideas through three types of evolutive thinking. E is for Evolve, and we covered the business element of it in the last chapter. Part two of Evolve is the personal bit, so this chapter is concerned with your personal happiness. As I mentioned earlier, there is no point in 'fixing' the business when you are not content yourself. So now we are going to force you to bare your soul (don't worry, you can do it in private if you want) so that you can accurately reconcile your working life with your personal wishes and aspirations. The process has five parts – four sets of questions you need to answer, and a concluding summary. So let's start.

Part I: What am I like?

This is an exercise that I have often run in training sessions. Take a sheet of paper and write the question What am I like? at the top. Take ten minutes or so to write down your thoughts. This is supposed to be an honest assessment of how you come across. You can produce a series of notes, or a flow of observations, so long as it is what you genuinely think you are like. If relevant, you can highlight distinctions between how you think you come across, and how you really feel. If you have trouble doing this, try these questions.

- If someone met you for the first time, how would they describe you?
- How would you describe yourself to someone you have never met?
- Are there differences between your work and outside personality?
- Is your inner self significantly different from your outward persona?

Part II: Decide your own style

The previous exercise will have weeded out whether you are being unrealistic about yourself or not. If you have never thought about it before, you now have a description of yourself to consider. There may be elements of your style in it, or maybe not. If there aren't, or if you want to change how you come across, the next step is to define that style. Take another ten minutes to answer these questions.

- Who or what is your favourite person or team(s)?
- What qualities make them so good?
- How can those qualities inspire your approach?
- Now define your own personal style.

So now you have a personal assessment and a defined style in front of you. Put that aside for a moment. We will come back to it in a minute.

Part III: So what do I *really* want?

So now we know what you are like, and what style you would like to emulate. Now let's get to the heart of what is going to make you happy in life. Answer these rather direct and personal questions on a separate sheet of paper.

- What's the point of my life?
- Why do I bother working?
- What, ultimately, do I want for myself?
- By when?

This needs to be a very honest exercise. There is no point in deluding yourself because you are the potential beneficiary, or loser, depending on how you reply. Your orientation should be 'I do this because ...'.

Part IV: I pledge ...

Take another blank piece of paper and write at the top of it 'I pledge'. Now write down what you are going to do differently from now on in order to achieve what you want. If you can't articulate it in your own words, answer these three questions.

- How exactly am I going to get where I want to be?
- Do I need help and, if so, from whom?
- By when will I achieve this?

Part V: My Lifesmile Statement

You have now effectively written all the elements of your Lifesmile Statement. It should have four parts so far, and we will now complete it with a fifth – the summary. Collect the four pieces of paper you should now have, and put them together. If you prefer, type them all out on one sheet along the lines shown in Figure 7.

1 This is what I am like
2 This is my personal style
3 What I really want is
4 I pledge ...

All you have to do now is answer one final question.

5 If there's one thing I am going to do it is ...

This completes your Lifesmile Statement. Everything on it is designed to make you happy, and if you manage to do what it says, you certainly will be. So print it out, blow it up large and stick it on the wall to remind yourself every day what you are all about.

This is what I am like:

____

This is my personal style:

____

What I really want is:

____

I pledge:

____

If there's one thing I am going to do it is:

____

figure 7 my Lifesmile Statement

Part I: What am I like?

- If someone met you for the first time, how would they describe you?
- How would you describe yourself to someone you have never met?
- Are there differences between your work and outside personality?
- Is your inner self significantly different from your outward persona?

Part II: Decide your own style

- Who or what is your favourite person or team(s)?
- What qualities make them so good?
- How can those qualities inspire your approach?
- Now define your own personal style

Part III: What do I *really* want?

- What's the point of my life?
- Why do I bother working?
- What, ultimately, do I want for myself?
- By when?

Part IV: I pledge ...

- How exactly am I going to get where I want to be?
- Do I need help and, if so, from whom?
- By when will I achieve this?

Part V: My Lifesmile Statement

- If there's one thing I am going to do it is:

figure 8 complete Lifesmile Statement method

Try being angular

There are lots of ways to answer the questions we have just posed. If the answers come naturally to you, then move on to the next chapter or take a breather. These personal matters can be a bit harrowing sometimes. But if you developed writer's block, here are some suggestions to drag your opinions out of you. They are in there somewhere. You can try the same method that we used to determine the future of the business, by simply stating your one-year, three-year, five-year or ten-year aims for yourself. If not, be a bit more perverse. See if you agree or disagree with these assertions.

- To stay interesting, you have to stay angry.
- A happy owner means a good business.
- It is good to be conventionally odd.
- Big picture, small picture, forget the picture – it doesn't matter.
- Never apologize, never explain.

If you agree, write down why, and how you personally enact that approach. If you disagree, write down why, plus your alternative.

> **'I'm always doing things I can't do. That's how I get to do them.'** *Pablo Picasso*

Push yourself to have aspirations that are beyond what you currently do. It keeps you stimulated and increases your chances of success when you are growing your business, because interested students are more tenacious about their subject. In short, consider doing some things you have never done.

A board meeting with yourself

Another way of dealing with writer's block is to imagine having a board meeting with yourself. Of course, self-employed people do this all the time, and they are very used to mulling over conflicting thoughts on their own. It is a technique you can use when you have lots of colleagues too. Imagine you are in a board meeting, and that you are being subjected to intense questioning. Take the nastiest questions that you didn't fancy answering from the process in this chapter, and pretend that you absolutely have to answer. If you still can't produce anything ask a partner, close friend, or someone who knows nothin about your business, to force you to answer them.

'A fanatic is one who can't change his mind and won't change the subject.' *Winston Churchill*

Nailing a jelly to the wall

An exasperated colleague of mine once exclaimed: 'I'm trying t nail a jelly to the wall here'. Bear in mind that if something i vague, it's useless, so you must have clear statements about wha you desire for your future. Keep it clear and keep it fresh.

'When you've run out of red, use blue!' *Pablo Picasso*

You have now completed phase III. The tripwires should hav secured what you need to achieve on behalf of the business, an the Lifesmile Statement has articulated what you want as a individual. We could stop there, and by all means do. There is however, always the small matter of the unexpected, lurkin around every corner, to scupper even the best-laid plans. So, i you fancy it, phase IV deals with the thorny issue of *What next*

Chapter 8 recap

1. Have you clarified what you are like?
2. Have you decided your own style?
3. Have you written down what you really want?
4. Have you made some pledges?
5. If so, what are they?
6. Have you completed your Lifesmile Statement?
7. Have you tried some new angles?
8. Are you able to have a board meeting with yourself?
9. Is your plan clear and fresh?
10. Are you ready to pin it on the wall?

Cautionary Tale: Estelle Carradine, the nutritionist who didn't know when to turn business down

Nutrition is a strange area. Everybody needs it, but many wouldn't dream of paying for it. Estelle was a bright, thoroughly qualified expert who reckoned she could run a successful business in this field, but didn't want to get bogged down working for a massive organization such as the health service. She preferred the idea of an independent practice with high quality and large volume clients that would be prepared to pay a premium price.

The business model looked excellent, and she had no trouble attracting suitable outside investment. The numbers were predicated on her ability to build a business with 30 or more staff, with a limited number of high-ticket customers such as football clubs, airlines and corporations where the health and vitality of their top people was high up the agenda.

But although that was what was written in the business plan, it is not how the business developed at all. She became frustrated after three or four months that the business had not attracted the type of large customers that the plan had specified. Instead of being patient and sticking to the plan, which was a good one, she started to accept precisely the opposite sort of business – individuals with no known credit history, low likelihood of repeat purchase, and no economies of scale.

This behaviour led her staff to believe that this sort of customer was viable and desirable to the company, and soon enough that was indeed the nature of their client base. Larger corporate prospects looked at the small size of their customers and concluded that they were a small operation for individuals, and after two years she had to collapse the business back down to a one-person company and start again.

Estelle should have known to turn down inappropriate business at the beginning, and should have had the confidence to see her plan through.

phase IV
what next?

In this phase you will learn:

- **how not to confuse movement with progress**
- **that corporations don't have memories**
- **how to work out what to do next**

The fourth and final phase of the CHEW system is What next? It is deliberately posed as a question because we have already agreed that we cannot be too prescriptive about growth, and that it can take many forms. All the thinking in the world cannot legislate for what life may throw at us, so the best preparation for those vicissitudes is to assume that nothing will go as planned, and take it from there.

What next? (quizzical phrase): to question the future, immediate or long-term

We already saw in chapter 2 that an optimist sees an opportunity in every calamity, and part of the knack with this is guessing the landscape and the possible outcomes in advance. If you can master the art of realizing that things will go wrong *before* they go wrong, then you are half way there. We will deal with this in three chapters. Chapter 9 says that you mustn't confuse movement with progress. This is all about the problem of rushing about conveying the semblance of action when in fact no progress is being made. Chapter 10 deals with the fact that corporations don't have memories – they are made up of constantly moving sets of individuals, which can cause difficulties when you think you have a long-term loyal customer, and then discover one day that you don't. And the final chapter discusses in a light-hearted way how everything may or may not be related to everything else. This is to get you thinking in a more general way about cause and effect.

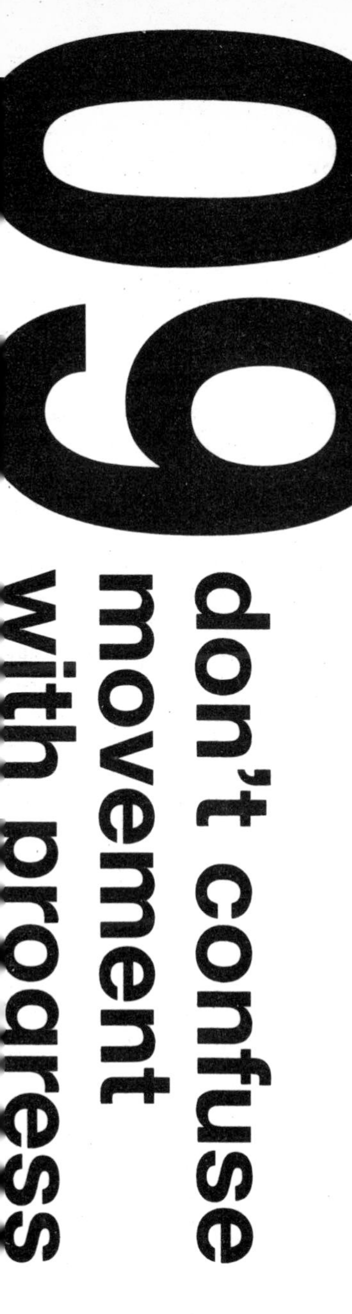

09 don't confuse movement with progress

In this chapter you will learn:

- how not to confuse movement with progress
- how to concentrate on action, not activity
- how to concentrate on outcome, not output
- how to identify and avoid obfuscation
- that business does not have to mean being busy

Much ado about nothing. Lots of movement but no forward motion. All talk and no action. How many times have you observed in life that a lot *appears* to be happening, but in fact, nothing much really is? That is what this chapter is all about. If you run a business, or wish to grow one successfully, then you haven't got the time, nor probably the patience, to allow people to faff about, or events to drift along, when what they are doing has no particular bearing on the main point. It is what the Italians call the English Disease: rushing around creating the *impression* that things are happening, but with no real tangible results.

Before I continue, I need to acknowledge the inspiration behind the chapter's title. My brother has a friend who is an experienced diplomat. They were driving on the motorway one day when an overtaking car sped rapidly into a gap just in front of them. The diplomat, an experienced pilot as well as a highly competent driver, declared: 'Don't confuse movement with progress'. The moral lies in an ability to move towards the intended objective without undue histrionics which, although they create the impression of activity, have no true bearing on the ultimate outcome. This is a vital lesson for anyone in business. Let's have a look at some other ways of phrasing it.

- Commando raids are good. Carpet bombing isn't.
- Laser strikes are good. Detonating everything isn't.
- Specific things are good. Generating lots of stuff to do isn't.
- Orderly progress to an intended destination is good. Buzzing around like a fly in a bottle isn't.
- It is better to arrive quietly than to make a big noise trying to get there.

This last one sounds like an ancient Chinese proverb, but it isn't. I just made it up. But you get the idea. Do not allow yourself to be fooled by a smokescreen of activity when you know very well it is simply to disguise the fact that the main item is not being done.

Action not activity

A lot of modern business people think that they are really clever if they are busy. I disagree. The smart operator knows how to have things working for them. What's so clever about being busy? All you need is a certain amount of activity to keep you stimulated, leaving the remainder of the time for you to pursue the things that really matter to you. Any fool can appear to be permanently busy. If you ring someone for an appointment and they can offer you a 'window of opportunity' in six months' time, then there are two possible explanations. The first is that they are hugely in demand, and thoroughly enjoying every second of it. In which case, good luck to them. The second (more likely) reason is that they are not in control of their own life and have too many meetings discussing stuff that doesn't have much bearing on the main point. Which applies to you?

From the training sessions that I have run over the last few years, I have learnt that the average amount of time that people in service industries spend bogged down in meetings is between 40 and 60 per cent of their working week. This figure is staggering. When you consider that the majority of meetings are to discuss *how* to move something forward, this statistic begs the question of *when* exactly these people are supposed to find the time to enact all the things that are raised in these apparently highly important meetings. If you want something to happen, concentrate on the action, not on activity that makes it look as though action is occurring.

Outcome not output

Meetings are not the only culprit in this context. In many corporations, bureaucracy is endemic. So often they make it look as though something is happening, when frequently it isn't. The output of an organization really doesn't matter much. It is the outcome that matters. If you achieve something excellent, who cares how you got there? If you have a great idea, who cares whether it happened in a flash, or over two weeks, or several years? Can you imagine someone saying: 'What a great idea. I wonder how many meetings they needed to make that happen?' I don't think so. Here is a list of business activities that, more often than not, are a waste of time.

- Meetings
- Conference calls
- Status reports
- Reports
- Travelling
- Communal emails

I can hear you exclaiming now. He is completely wrong! We couldn't function without these things! But look again, and you will see that I have said 'more often than not'. This is the point. With some careful thought and application, you should be able to reduce your output by half, so that you can concentrate on the outcome. Try asking yourself some of these questions.

- Do I really need to have that meeting?
- Does it need to be that long?
- Do all those people need to be there?
- Do I need this piece of paperwork?
- Does anyone else?
- Does that need to be written down?
- Do I need to send that email?
- Do I need to have that conversation?
- Does that even need to be discussed?

There are hundreds of questions that can change your working life. In chapter 5, we looked at Lee Iacocca saying: 'They tell me what they think. Then I decide.' If you are good at business, you weigh up the situation, make a decision, and then get on with it. It can save hours, days, even years of hanging about. So the best question of all is:

- Can we just get on with it?

This question will blow the doors off most government departments and have millions of big corporate citizens dashing to their subsidized canteens for a cheap cappuccino. You see, most people *want* to look busy, regardless of whether there is an outcome. Don't let that person be you.

The art of obfuscation

There will be plenty reading this who will think that the author has gone a bit barmy at this point, but bear with me. Have you ever heard of obfuscation?

> **Obfuscation** (noun): the act or an instance of making something deliberately obscure or difficult to understand

It's not quite the same as time wasting. It is nothing to do with being idle or unintelligent. No, it is much smarter than that. It is about making something appear more complicated than it truly is, or needs to be. Lots of professions do it all the time. People have to hire lawyers because they have surrounded themselves with a language that no one else can understand. City traders are the same. Most industries have a jargon that provides a force field that is designed to exclude everyone else. That enables them to appear clever, and to cast a veil over their activities. That in turn allows them to charge more for their services and generally feel superior. All industries do it. It isn't even a particularly evil activity. It seems to happen naturally. You know the kind of thing.

> *'Jane was talking to Dave about the ZXC. Of course, he said it was ludicrous that the project manager never filled in the 87-K, and now that LOD have got hold of it, it'll probably be sent to the pit bulls in back-end architecture or thrown into the hands of AWOB with the rest of the ideas from Project Azalea.'*

Impenetrable rubbish, I am sure you will agree. Under no circumstances should you ever end up talking like this. It undermines your credibility and makes you sound less intelligent than you are. If you remain unconvinced that there is too much language in business that encourages confusion, have a look at the range of phrases in use to describe unnecessary talk.

Blather (Scottish; blether): foolish talk; nonsense
Drivel: unintelligible language
Hot air: empty talk
Jabber: to speak without making sense
Nonsense: something that makes no sense
Piffle: nonsense
Rabbit: to talk inconsequentially
Static: interference in transmissions
Verbiage: excessive and often meaningless use of words
Waffle: to speak in a vague and wordy manner
Whim-wham: something fanciful; a trifle
White noise: sound with wide continuous range of frequencies of uniform intensity

I have barely scratched the surface. The list goes on and on, and the descriptive vocabulary for this phenomenon is so rich precisely *because* it is such a frequent occurrence. But be under no illusion: if you want to get something done, you haven't got time for this sort of prevarication. Life is not that complicated, and business certainly doesn't have to be.

> **'There cannot be a crisis next week. My schedule is already full.'** *Henry Kissinger*

You will have heard the axiom that work expands to fit the time available in which to do it. The alternative, of course, is that you are too busy to create the time for anything else. Neither extreme makes any sense. Why surround yourself with irrelevant things to do, when you have lots of other genuinely interesting things to do? Something of a rhetorical question perhaps, but we all have examples of circumstances in which nothing important is getting done because too much irrelevant stuff is being done instead. If you suspect that this might be the case with your business, or with any of your customers, then you have some serious thinking to do.

Business does not mean being busy

Busy used to mean (literally) being actively or fully engaged, and there's nothing wrong with that. But it has also come to mean overcrowded with detail, and that is not a good thing. Never confuse movement with progress. Work out the bits that matter, and do them only. If you have spare time, do something you want to do in order to ensure your sustained happiness, not something that supports the idea that you are frantically busy. Try these phrases to puncture the idea that being busy is beneficial.

- Claiming to be too busy is the last refuge of an ailing business person.
- Being busy used to be macho – now it is gender neutral.
- If you are too busy, you have no time for yourself.
- If you are too busy, you have no time for anyone else.
- If you are too busy, you are one-dimensional.
- If you are too busy, you are missing the point.

- If you are too busy, you are missing out on life.
- If you are too busy, you are incompetent.

There's a tidal wave coming. Here's a paper cup

Many people in business feel that they are under-equipped to deal with what life is going to throw at them. They feel as though they have been given a paper cup, and told that there is a tidal wave coming. But coping with business, or 'busyness', is all about guessing the landscape and the possible outcomes *before* they occur. This is not nearly as difficult as you might think. The first step is to realize that things may well go wrong *before* they go wrong. That's not a particularly complicated idea now is it? Put even more simply, assume the worst, and do your best. Life's a mess. Adapt. Be prepared for changes and make it up as you go along. Plan B is often better than Plan A. (The idea of plan B being more productive than plan A is discussed in *Teach Yourself Running your own Business*, page 93.) Stick to the simple stuff, and don't let administration and bureaucracy get in the way. If you view business as a nasty tidal wave, then your perspective needs some adjustment. Try asking yourself these questions.

- What is likely to happen?
- When?
- What can I do to anticipate that?
- What can I do to prepare for that?
- What can I do to influence that?
- What can I do to prevent that?
- What can I do to make that tolerable?

It is a form of disaster planning, except that these are not disasters. They are just the normal nuisances that happen in business every day.

> **'A change of nuisances is as good as a holiday.'**
>
> *David Lloyd George*

Everything busier than everything else

Don't confuse movement with progress. The illusion that things will be better when they are busier needs careful consideration, because it doesn't make any sense. Do you really agree with the idea that if there is a lot happening, then progress is being made? The old joke goes that when marketing activity does not have the desired effect, Marketing Directors immediately do more of it. Instead, they would be better placed to work out why it didn't work first, and then make their next move. What do politicians do when they see light at the end of the tunnel? Order more tunnel! So before you rush around like a headless chicken without knowing why, ask yourself these questions.

- Why am I doing this?
- What's wrong with things as they are?
- Will the proposed activity get me anywhere?
- Is this worth doing?
- Why?
- What is the likely return in relation to my efforts?
- Is this the beginning, the middle or the end of the sequence?
- Do I need to rethink this?

At the heart of all this is the maxim: Never do anything unless you know why you are doing it (this is on page 91 of *Teach Yourself Running your own Business*). No one is proposing that you become idle – simply that you do not fool yourself into believing that all the rushing around you are doing is achieving anything, unless of course you have genuinely worked out that it definitely is. In which case, move on to the next chapter immediately.

Chapter 9 recap

1. Have you confused movement with progress?
2. Have you banished activity in favour of action?
3. Can you spot obfuscation?
4. If so, what have you done to eradicate it?
5. Have you reduced the amount of bureaucracy in your life?
6. Have you asked why you can't just get on with it?
7. Do you often claim to be too busy?
8. Is it really true?
9. Have you anticipated what is likely to happen *before* it does?
10. Ask again: why am I doing this?

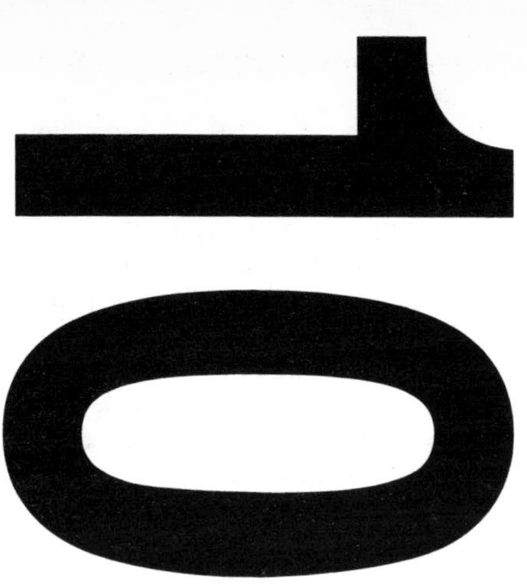

10 corporations don't have memories

In this chapter you will learn:

- **that corporations don't have memories**
- **that corporations are just clusters of individuals**
- **that history does not repeat itself**
- **that your relationships probably aren't**
- **how to overcome corporate amnesia, apathy and aggression**

We have looked at the confusion created by displacement activity. That is something that you, and your colleagues if you have them, can self-generate, to your own detriment. But what about the behaviour of your customers? Now let's move on to look at how you can understand better the phenomena that drive your customer relationships. There are hundreds of books about customer retention, and they are all predicated on the basis that it is good to keep customers. There's nothing wrong with that, but what happens when your customer suddenly isn't? You see, corporations don't have memories. They are made up of constantly moving sets of individuals, which can cause difficulties when you think that you have a long-term loyal customer, and then suddenly discover that you don't. Those who do business with large corporations love to be associated with them. It makes them sound important, and gives clues as to their quality with other potential customers. But, apart from a few of the largest contracts in the world, most business is conducted between clusters of individuals which means that, if they change, then so does the relationship. And that could mean that there no longer is one.

History does not repeat itself

There is a common notion that history often repeats itself. Shirley Bassey certainly sang about it at length, but I think that it is nonsense. As a species, man has a spectacular track record of 'unlearning' all sorts of skills. You only have to look at a few ancient civilizations to spot that. So information and knowledge is by no means always passed down, and that can cause all sorts of problems for businesses that desire a long-term relationship with a particular customer.

> **'History does not repeat itself. At best it sometimes rhymes.'**
>
> *Mark Twain*

Of course, similar things do happen over time. But is this because people have deliberately engineered it, or because they are making the same mistakes another time? Part of the problem revolves around the manner in which history is recorded. We all know that politicians, military men, writers and so on all like to express events on their own terms, and people in business do it too. In chapter 4, page 47, we discussed the idea that you should always admit if something was a fluke, otherwise you would delude yourself into thinking that you had orchestrated the success. Well, people in business love rewriting history too. That's because it makes them look better. If you want a pay rise, then summarize the last couple of years as a relentless period of progress, and you may well get one. Everyone likes to make it look as though they made clinical strategic decisions to influence a situation for the better, when frequently those things were going to happen anyway.

> **'History is not what you thought. It is what you can remember.'** *W. C. Sellar*

So history can easily be rewritten and, often, it is rewritten in front of your very eyes. This may or may not bother you in a global context, but it might if it refers to business issues that have a deep and immediate bearing on your welfare and happiness. Let's take an example. You or your company starts working for a large corporation with, say, over 3,000 staff. You have a main contact, in charge of procurement, and get to meet three or four other less senior characters as you work on the first project. That goes well, so over the next three years you win more and more work, to the point where this customer accounts for 65 per cent of your income, and 60 per cent of your profit. All is seemingly rosy, but then things start to happen. Your main contact is moving on. They might have been fired. They might be retiring. They might be moving to another division, or overseas. The reason doesn't matter. They remain a great fan of you and your work, but they aren't there any more to sign off the money. For a while, there is no replacement. Their subordinates can authorize a limited amount of other work, but the main stuff is put on hold until a successor arrives. One of the team goes on maternity leave. The successor arrives, and won't take a meeting with you because they have too much else to do, and you have never met before. They bring in their own team and start working with someone else. Without so much as a conversation, you have lost two-thirds of your business.

Corporations: just clusters of individuals

Time was, you took your job as a trainee at the bank, and 50 years later you collected your commemorative gold watch at your retirement bash. Not any more. People come and go with alarming regularity, and that means your customers can move at the same speed, because they are effectively the same people. In marketing, the average length of time that someone spends in a job is 18 months. This is just enough time to:

- Fail to understand the job properly
- Deny all responsibility for previous events
- Initiate a few things on scanty information
- Leave before they are finished, thereby avoiding responsibility for any outcome.

I exaggerate to make a point, but you get the idea. Now translate this from a personal level to the one that could affect the relationship between your company and theirs. Your new customer may only be around long enough to:

- Grasp a vague notion of what you do
- Put a few things in train with your company
- Fail to inform colleagues of the extent of your capabilities
- Move on to somewhere else.

That is a chain of events that could occur even with the best will and the most decent person in the world. It's not personal – it's just business. Even worse, their successor could:

- Fail to understand what you do properly
- Show disinterest in all previous work
- Not bother to take a meeting with you
- Use previous contacts to replace you for similar work
- Unwittingly destroy your business.

Your relationships aren't

So you are faced with the constantly moving customer. Once you have got the hang of this, you will be forced to admit that your relationships aren't.

> **'Firings will continue until morale improves.'** *Anonymous*

People are cheap these days, and loyalty is a rare thing. They get fired, you get fired. It's as simple as that. Many people running businesses reckon that they are only one phone call away from disaster. If the call comes, they are going to be making redundancies or folding the business. So let's have a look at some of the things that can be done to alleviate this sort of problem when it arises, as it inevitably will one day.

Overcoming corporate amnesia

'Sorry, who are you?' You can hear the phone call now, and it won't be that pleasant. Your major customer doesn't know who you are. So how do you ingratiate yourself so that they do remain a customer? Here are some ideas.

- **Be more organized than they are.** When people arrive new in a job, it is difficult for them to know what to do next. If you are efficient and well organized, you can become very useful to them and help them along. Let them know how, and look for an opportunity to prove it.
- **Keep records.** In certain businesses, customers have no idea where their predecessor kept the information on a certain subject. Frequently, knowledge is lost on the way. If you have it, you need to let them know, and use your knowledge of their business to your advantage. History may not repeat itself, but something will have been learnt on the way.
- **Anticipate seasonal variations.** A lot of businesses are seasonal, which means that contact with customers could be scarce in the low season. If this applies to your business, then anticipate the periods of minimal contact, and do something about it. For example, if you conduct business with them intensively over the summer, then deliberately arrange to meet in December to stay in touch.
- **Use case histories.** Write up and analyse the success and value of what you have already done for the customer. Quantify it. Show where improvements can be made. Then add lots of new ideas.

> **'Nothing has really happened until it has been described.'**
>
> *Virginia Woolf*

Overcoming corporate apathy

Let's say that the customer hasn't forgotten who you are. Instead, they are indifferent about hearing what you have to offer. Try some of these approaches.

- **Rip it up and start again.** Pretend you have never had this customer, and start again. Use all the enthusiasm of a new kid on the block, attack the subject with a new perspective, and propose a meeting to reveal it all.
- **Reinvent yourself.** It is of course possible that you personally are a bit jaded when it comes to this customer. If that is true, then consider introducing a colleague to the mix to replicate the conditions of a new relationship.
- **Do something imaginative.** Introduce fresh ideas. Do not attach yourself too heavily to the past. The new person doesn't care what went on before, unless it has a direct bearing on their fortunes now. In which case, tell them straightaway what worked previously, but do remember that the past is not very interesting to most people in business. It is the future that they are worried about.

> **'Never let yesterday use up too much of today.'** *Will Rogers*

Overcoming corporate aggression

Sometimes people can be downright hostile. Without going into all the potential psychological reasons for this (you know the sort of stuff – insufficient potty training; hamster drowned as a child; Napoleon syndrome), there are quite a few things you can do to soften up their brusque attitude. Try some of these.

- **Be completely objective about past performance.** If your properties were found wanting in the past, then say so – your competitors will be the first to point out your deficiencies. If your people have been weak or inconsistent, admit it and remedy it. If your attitude or keenness has fluctuated, explain why and offer solutions. Have they had value for money? View it as though you were the customer and be honest. If any elements simply weren't good enough, say so – hindsight should enable you to depersonalize it.
- **Produce an honest analysis of your strengths versus the competition.** Don't say you are better than your competitors at everything – it is very unlikely to be true. Claim a mixture

of skills that appears to be objective or use impartial external data. This will enable you to highlight subtly any competitor weaknesses and draw out your own strengths.

- **Quantify the cost of moving.** Outline any time lags on work already underway. Consider the effect of your notice period and finishing up work in progress. Quantify the start-up time needed for them to get a new relationship in train with someone else. Do a calculation totalling their investment in briefing and meeting time, and the required learning curve. Try to find an industry survey that shows that anyone moving their business has to increase effectiveness by x per cent just to cover their investment in the move.
- **Ask directly what reservations they have.** Listen hard! This is no time to pretend everything is fine, because if it were they would not be reviewing the business. Drag out all their concerns and address them. Be sure to let them invent their own solutions if they make sense, because they will be more likely to go with those options if they think that they had the ideas themselves.

So there you have it. Take a careful look at your customer base. If you conclude that you are relying too heavily on one or two large customers, consider how those relationships could go wrong long before they do, and take the sorts of steps we have discussed in this chapter. The ideas are not designed to scare you senseless, and you certainly should not spend endless nights worrying about the possibility of losing a major customer. Just consider the possibilities, and do something about it now.

Chapter 10 recap

1. Have you learnt anything from the past?
2. How are you going to apply that learning?
3. Are you guilty of rewriting history?
4. Have you anticipated relationships that could go wrong?
5. What have you done about that?
6. Have you considered ways to overcome corporate amnesia, apathy or aggression?
7. Are you more organized than your customers?
8. Are you capable of reinventing yourself?
9. Are you honest about yourself in relation to the competition?
10. Have you been totally objective about past performance?

everything may or may not be related to everything else

In this chapter you will learn:

- **that everything may or may not be related to everything else**
- **how to thrive on chaos**
- **how action can lead to chain reaction**
- **that everything changes all the time**
- **to ask yourself regularly whether you have actually done it**

For those of you who are reading this end-to-end, we have now arrived at the final part. In phase I, Confront, we faced up to the realities of your business and asked some tricky questions such as *What now?* and *Are you disciplined enough to be free?* Then we went on to look at freedom of thought. In phase II, Hone, we introduced the Foo fighting system, and three types of evolutive thinking: the facts, your own opinion, and other people's wisdom. There was much to learn from the survey, and hopefully you should have been able to apply large chunks of it to your circumstances.

Phase III, Evolve, encouraged you to set up your business tripwires and drop some grenades in fishponds, and to resolve your personal perspective by writing your own Lifesmile Statement. In Phase IV, What next?, we have wrestled with the unpredictable vagaries of business life. *Don't confuse movement with progress* dealt with the pitfalls of obfuscation, and recommended action not activity, outcome not output. And we have just dealt with the problem that corporations don't have memories. So now we will finish off with a light-hearted look at how everything may or may not be related to everything else.

'Butterfly destroys city': chaos theory revisited

Everything may or may not be related to everything else. Cause and effect is a well-established concept. In one extreme example, a butterfly landing on a tree in a rainforest in South America leads to a chain of events that sees a city destroyed by a hurricane thousands of miles away. At a more personal level, if I do x, then y will probably happen. It all makes perfect sense. And yet, people believe just as much in chance, superstition, fate, and a whole range of other ideas that are essentially random. So *can* you predict what is going to happen to you or your business? Or does it all just occur anyway?

> **Chaos theory** (noun): a theory, applied in various branches of science, that apparently random phenomena have underlying order

Now there's a heavy concept. Chaos theory is suggesting that, even though everything looks as though it is happening randomly, it actually has some sort of order. This is not a philosophy book, so I don't think we need to spend time diligently presenting the pros and cons, but it certainly is a big idea. So does that mean that everything in your business is related to everything else? Well, it might do, but then again it might not.

Action and chain reaction

Most actions lead to a reaction, and if pushed to the furthest degree, that will become a chain reaction. The question is whether this matters or not. Well, it might matter on three counts.

1 You want something to happen as a result of your actions.
2 You do not want something to happen as a result of your actions.
3 You don't know what will happen as a result of your actions.

It all boils down to:

> If I do x, they will do y. Do I want this to happen?

If you are in position number one, then go ahead and do whatever you want to do. If it is number two, then you need to think hard about whether you really do want to do it, or what contingency plans you have in mind. If it is scenario three, then you probably haven't thought about it enough, so pause and think.

> **'Very few things happen at the right time, and the rest do not happen at all. The conscientious historian will correct these defects.'** *Heroditus*

If you are not much of a fan of the cause and effect principle, you nevertheless have to cope with stuff happening. The sequence in which it happens is immaterial – how are you going to deal with it all? As Heroditus points out, very few things happen at the right time. The more experienced people become when running businesses, the more they conclude that very few things have a predictable pattern. Just when you think they do, they don't. That means that you usually have to make it up as you go along. He also points out that most things do not happen at 'the right time'. For a full rundown on understanding time, have a look at *Teach Yourself Running your own Business*, chapter 6. Suffice to say, you cannot plan a business on supposition, and some would say that you can barely plan at all.

Everything changes

I was once taking a short break in Ireland, and I wandered into a newsagent to buy a paper. As I walked out of the door, the owner called after me, 'Come back tomorrow, there'll be more news then'.

The remark has always stuck with me. Apart from being very funny, it is also highly perspicacious when it comes to the recurring nature of news, or events. There is always more news. That applies to businesses just as much as every other aspect of life. So, assume there will be more news to deal with, and roll with it. There is great merit in planning, as many parts of this book advocate, but you have to be flexible. Here is a rough sequence that the flexible business person should follow.

- Plan it
- Do it
- Change it
- Do it differently.

This applies equally to your own subject matter as it does to the manner in which you might wish to react to competitive manoeuvres. Zig when they zag is a common strategy for constantly staying distinctive in relation to your competitors. In the new ultra-flexible world, this could be updated to zig when they zag, and then zog.

It's all in your mind

> **'Half this game is ninety per cent mental.'**
>
> *Philadelphia Phillies manager Danny Ozark*

Of course we have all had some fun at the expense of sports managers and commentators for the way they trip over their words. And yet there is always a truism lurking beneath the gobbledegook. Much of it is to do with aspects of psychology, and many are transferable to a business context. For example, many coaches refuse to discuss the opposition because they are not interested in adapting their way of playing to allow for their opponents' system. They want it to happen the other way round. 'Never discuss the competition' is an interesting maxim, and there are even examples of 'uncompetitive reviews', where the business is reviewed but the competition is not allowed to be discussed for fear of diluting exciting ideas with too much knowledge. Here is another essential weapon in your mental armoury.

- Do I value their opinion?

It is a very powerful question. If someone says something that disturbs you, or with which you do not agree, ask yourself whether you value their opinion. If not, move on and don't lose sleep over it. Only pay attention to observations from a source that you intrinsically respect. Your confidence and happiness are all relative, and they are all in the mind.

Yes, but have you actually done it?

We talked in chapter 7 about the difference between something being underway and it actually being finished. There are all sorts of ideas in this book, and hopefully they will have triggered many more. But none of them are any use to you unless you actually do some of them. So, if you have been drifting through this book and thinking, 'That's a good idea', then now is the time to get on with it. An idea is only as good as its implementation.

Closing remarks

'How can I conclude until I hear what I have to say?' *Anon*

My father was once sitting in a formal Air Force presentation at which a senior dignitary was droning on. Someone at the back, risking a court martial or some other heinous punishment, muttered, 'Come to the point.' Against all the odds, the speaker heard the remark, looked up from behind his half-moon spectacles, and responded to the heckler. 'How can I conclude until I hear what I have to say?' A brilliant riposte for sure, and a moral lies within. Make sure you take the time to hear yourself out. That has been the theme of this book. Growing your business, if that is what you wish for, is all about careful thought. Give yourself the thinking time that you deserve and need in order to achieve a decent result.

> **'Somebody's boring me. I think it's me.'** *Dylan Thomas*

Equally, don't drag it out for ages. Some careful thought is good. Paralysis by analysis is not. Get the conditions right. Consider the wider context. Scour the CHEW system for some techniques that you like. Pick and choose the bits that work for you, but don't be slavish about it. Try some evolutive thinking. Whittle it down to the elements that you think are going to help. Make sure you keep your personal interests firmly at the centre of it. Don't get distracted or knocked off course by extraneous factors. Just get on and do it. That's it. Now, before I outstay my welcome, I am going to stop. Off you go then, and good luck.

> **'Nothing is my last word on anything.'** *Henry James*

Chapter 11 recap

1 What do you think: are things related?
2 If so, can you determine cause and effect?
3 If not, how are you going to deal with random events?
4 Have you got your head straight?
5 Have you set aside some decent thinking time?
6 Have you applied some interesting techniques?
7 What did your thinking reveal?
8 Have you actually done what you decided to?
9 Have you considered yourself in all of this?
10 Do you feel reinvigorated?

Appendix 1: 110 pieces of other people's wisdom

How to develop your business successfully

1 Have a clear understanding of why your business exists
2 Work hard on motivation
3 Be patient
4 Nurture contacts carefully
5 Take the plunge and take risks
6 Learn to let go of some things
7 Use your partners judiciously
8 Find brave customers
9 Grow prudently
10 Keep an eye on escalating bureaucracy
11 Spend the time to find the right people and build the right team
12 Remember different skills are required to set up a business than to grow one
13 You don't have to win by much to win by a lot
14 Save today's income for tomorrow's expansion
15 Avoid going after everything that moves
16 Only acquire businesses to add skill sets you do not already have
17 Find the time to invest in growth
18 If you're not an interesting person, people won't want to do business with you

The Guide to Growth

1. To stay as you are is impossible
2. Momentum is important but size in itself is not
3. There is good growth and bad growth
4. Bad growth is doing things for the wrong reasons
5. Growth is good so long as it is profitable
6. Growth usually involves making a lot of mistakes
7. Work out how much money you want to extract and over what time period
8. Make sure quality of service is maintained
9. Do not pursue growth for growth's sake
10. Top up your leaky bucket constantly
11. Differentiate between higher turnover and better margin
12. Rapid growth can endanger quality and reputation
13. Know when to turn down business
14. A principle isn't a principle until it costs you money
15. Turnover or revenue is vanity, profit is sanity
16. Do not compromise what you set out to achieve in the first place
17. Don't change the thing that most clients like
18. Don't grow too fast and dilute what enabled you to grow in the first place

Beating the blues

1. Regard a launch as the beginning of the beginning rather than the end of the beginning
2. Tell yourself in advance that the honeymoon period will end
3. Continually question what your business does and how well it does it
4. Keep transforming it into a shinier, newer version of itself
5. Entrepreneurs are often good 'starters' or 'creators' but poor at routine
6. Work out how to deal with the highs and lows
7. Give yourself credit for what you have already achieved
8. Remind yourself why you're doing it
9. You and your partners have to evolve along with your business
10. Remember that most people in business have itchy and low times
11. Be aware that partners get the blues too, so act sensitively

12 Have the idea, build the car, then employ someone else to drive it for you
13 Realize that the business will never be 'finished'
14 Launching a business is a bit like having a baby
15 Running it can be like the loneliness of the long distance runner
16 Get a good non-exec to offer a different, less emotional perspective

How to plan the next big thing

1 Have an idea where you want to go but always be open to other opportunities
2 Talk to people who know more about it than you do and hear about their lives
3 Make quick decisions about opportunities that could influence your growth
4 Go for a long walk, or a run, get on the running machine, or in the shower
5 You only need to be five minutes ahead of the pack to succeed
6 Keep your big picture clear and at the forefront of everything you do
7 Ask your team
8 Keep lifting your head up and be ready to take opportunities
9 Always have a pen and paper handy
10 Make time for planning
11 Reinvent your business all the time
12 Listen to your customers and bright people
13 Look how successful businesses manage expansion in other sectors
14 Listen to what is happening around you
15 Allow yourself the time away to contemplate 'what else?'
16 Start with the people and the casting
17 Have an annual day of reflection
18 Be spurred on by ambitions that are way beyond your current reach
19 Get away from the business to have enlightening moments of inspiration
20 Use external consultants or facilitators to move into novel related areas

If I'd known this when I started ...

1 Plan and test everything before you set up
2 Be confident and have a clear picture of your worth
3 Equity is forever. Be very careful to whom you give equity
4 Everything takes a lot longer than you think
5 Make sure you're prepared for the rollercoaster ride
6 Networking is essential as talent alone in some cases is not enough
7 Invest in friendships and relationships – the rest will happen naturally
8 Understand the selling points which trigger income-generating responses
9 Listen to your gut feeling – it's usually right
10 All businesses are people businesses
11 Everyone running a business goes through some big lows
12 Few other people are as excited by your business or as committed as you are
13 Your customers know less about your subject matter than you do
14 Business is not personal
15 Your first instincts are normally right
16 Everything is negotiable
17 Always act and tell the truth fast
18 Talented craftsmen are by no means talented managers
19 Don't keep pursuing something if it isn't a success
20 If *you* don't do it, you don't get paid

Pass it on

1 You have to love what you do
2 Be absolutely clear about what your product or service is
3 Greed is usually transparent
4 You're probably better than you think you are – don't sell yourself too cheap
5 There are some people it's just not worth trying with
6 Enjoy the process of building the business, not just the dream of what you will one day achieve
7 Be brave, say what you really think, and go to bed knowing you did your best
8 Make mistakes and learn

9. Don't be afraid to move on from something if it is not working
10. Be with the people you enjoy being with
11. Reputation in any market is worth more than anything else
12. Never be afraid to ask advice from someone you admire
13. Do the important things first – don't put them off
14. Treat all people as you would expect to be treated yourself
15. Believe in what you are doing and at the same time listen to healthy criticism
16. Past success doesn't mean future success
17. Have Big Audacious Goals
18. Reach for the stars

Appendix 2: Book synopses

The Tipping Point, Malcolm Gladwell

What the books says

- Little things can make a big difference.
- Explains and defines the 'tipping point' – the moment at which ideas, trends and social behaviour cross a threshold, tip and spread like wildfire.
- Just as one sick person can start an epidemic, very minor adjustments to products or ideas can make them far more likely to be a success.
- The overall message of the book is that, contrary to the belief that big results require big efforts that are beyond the capacity of the single individual, one imaginative person applying a well-placed lever can move the world.

What's good about it

- It is optimistic in outlook and suggests that individuals can make a significant contribution. It cites the example of Paul Revere who, in 1775, overheard a conversation and rode all night to warn Americans in Boston that the British would attack in the morning. The Americans were ready and defeated them.
- The three areas (below) are a good working template for all communications:
  1. **The Law of the Few** – the idea that the nature of the messenger is critical.
  2. **The Stickiness Factor** – the quality of the message has to be good enough to be worth acting on.
  3. **The Power of Context** – people are exquisitely sensitive to changes of time, place and circumstance.

What you have to watch

- The three areas aren't that original – they are roughly similar to medium, message and target audience.
- It is easy to get distracted by the three groups of people who may start a tipping point: *Connectors* (people who know a lot of people), *Mavens* (those who accumulate knowledge, but are not persuaders), and *Salesmen* (people who are very persuasive).

- It is quite American, with many examples relating to the USA (for example, how removing graffiti reduced the crime rate in New York in the 1980s). Thought is needed with regard to application elsewhere.
- Even if a marketing strategy overtly sets out to create a tipping point, they are so idiosyncratic and hard to predict that it might not work.

How could this thinking be applied to your business?

Flicking Your Creative Switch, Wayne Lotherington

(more at: allsorts.com.au)

What the books says

- Everyone can be creative, regardless of whether they think they are.
- Creativity is variously described as 'the spark that ignites new ideas', 'the infinite capacity that resides within you', and 'shaping the game you play, not playing the game you find'.
- Good ideas arise when we take something we already know (light bulb no. 1) and consider it in relation to another thing we already know but which is unrelated (no. 2). Merging them creates light bulb number 3 – the new idea.

What's good about it

- It explains the origin of the phrase 'thinking outside the box'. The Gottschaldt figurine, or nine-dot game, requires you to join all the dots without taking your pen off the paper. You can't solve it if you view it as a box.
- ROI is used to stand for relevance, originality and impact. Your ideas won't work if they do not have all three.
- Barriers to creativity have been placed in our way since childhood: *don't be foolish, grow up, work before play, do as you're told, don't ask questions, obey the rules, be practical,* and so on.

- There are six techniques which you can use in any awayday to generate ideas:
  - **Random word:** take a noun randomly from somewhere and apply it to the subject. You can also use pictures.
  - **Eyes of experts:** choose three respected experts from other fields and consider how they would deal with your issue. There is a variation called Industrial Roundabout where you view it through a different category.
  - **What's hot?:** use popular current things to appeal to your audience.
  - **Curly questions:** use analogies, speculation, role reversal and imagination to re-phrase the issue at hand so that more original answers emerge.
  - **Exaggeration and depravation:** over-exaggerate the benefits of a product, or push to ludicrous extremes what happens if it isn't present.
  - **Exquisite corpse:** based on surrealist thinking, different people randomly select five words to create a sentence in the pattern adjective/noun/verb/adjective/noun. E.g. *The peculiar bicycle swims a brilliant banana.* Each word is then scrutinized to review the problem.

What you have to watch

- You need to control the exercises so they don't seem trivial.
- You need to be open-minded.

How could this thinking be applied to your business?

Eating the Big Fish, Adam Morgan

What the book says

- Most marketing books are written about brand leaders, but most marketing people don't work on brand leaders.
- These challenger brands need to behave differently if they are to compete with brand leaders – effectively doing more with less.

- There are eight credos:
  1 **Break with your immediate past** (forget everything you know and think again).
  2 **Build a lighthouse identity** (state what you are – don't reflect consumers).
  3 **Assume thought leadership of category** (the one everyone talks about).
  4 **Create symbols of re-evaluation** (do the unexpected).
  5 **Sacrifice** (work out what you are *not* going to do).
  6 **Overcommitment** (Karate experts aim two feet below the brick to break it).
  7 Use **advertising/publicity to enter popular culture.**
  8 **Become ideas-centred, not consumer-centred** (constantly re-invent).

What's good about it

- It concentrates on practical things that most brands can do.
- It tells you how to run a workshop and apply the thinking.
- Most of the credos can be used to overcome inertia.
- It can help small, under-resourced marketing teams to mobilize big ideas.
- Brand leaders can benefit from thinking like a challenger to stay number one.

What you have to watch

- It is easy to go round talking about 'creating a lighthouse identity' (and other phrases) without actually saying anything.
- Some of the ideas are easier said than done.
- Credo number 7 is easy to criticize because you would expect a communications expert to recommend activity.

How could this thinking be applied to your business?

The Pirate Inside, Adam Morgan

What the book says

- Powerful brands are built by people, not by proprietary methodologies.
- The real issue is not the strategy, but how we need to *behave* when an organization's systems seem more geared to slowing and diluting than spurring and galvanizing.
- To achieve this you need to be a *Constructive Pirate*. This is not the same as anarchy where there are 'no rules', but it requires a different *set* of rules.
- It shows how to write your own 'Articles' in your organization.
- Even in big organisations, you need challenger sub-cultures.

What's good about it

- It explains nine ways of behaving that stimulate challenger brand cultures:
  1. **Outlooking** – looking for different kinds of insights by:
     Emotional Insertion – Putting a new kind of emotion into the category
     Overlay – Overlaying the rules of a different category onto your own
     Brand Neighbourhoods – Radically re-framing your competitive set
     Grip – Finding a place for the brand to gain traction in contemporary culture.
  2. **Pushing** – Pushing ideas well beyond the norm.
  3. **Projecting** – Being consistent across far more media than the usual.
  4. **Wrapping** – Communicating less conventionally with customers.
  5. **Denting** – Respecting colleagues whilst making a real difference.
  6. **Binding** – Having a contract that ensures everyone comes with the idea.
  7. **Leaning** – Pushing harder for sustained commitment.
  8. **Refusing** – Having the passion to say no.
  9. **Taking It Personally** – A different professionalism that transcends corporate man.
- *Biting the Other Generals* is a good concept based on an anecdote from the Seven Years War. A brilliantly

unconventional general, James Wolfe, proved himself one of the most talented military leaders King George III had. When some of Wolfe's detractors tried to undermine him by complaining that he was mad, the king replied: 'Oh, he is mad, is he? Then I would he would bite some other of my generals.'
- *The Three Buckets* is a good exercise whereby you have to categorize all your existing projects into *Brilliant Basics, Compelling Differences* and *Changing the Game* – usually with poignant results.

What you have to watch

- Not much. This is an excellent book and you can use the exercises with pretty much any business.

How could this thinking be applied to your business?

Blink, Malcolm Gladwell

What the book says

- Our ability to 'know' something in a split-second judgement, without really knowing why we know, is one of the most powerful abilities we possess.
- A snap judgement made very quickly can actually be far more effective than one we make deliberately and cautiously.
- By blocking out what is irrelevant and focusing on narrow slices of experience, we can read seemingly complex situations in the blink of eye.
- This is essentially 'thinking without thinking'.
- He introduces the theory of 'thin slicing' – using the first two seconds of any encounter to determine intuitively your response or the likely outcome.
- He demonstrates that this 'little bit of knowledge' can go a long way, and is accurate in over 80 per cent of instances.

What's good about it

- There are scores of vivid examples in which people's first instincts have been right, but they cannot explain why. These include an art dealer identifying a fake statue that the Getty museum believes to be genuine, a tennis coach being able to predict every time when players are about to serve a double fault, and a psychologist accurately guessing years in advance if married couples will stay together or not.
- The thinking is a welcome counterpoint to a world in which too much reliance on proof and data has replaced hunch and instinct.
- The value of spontaneity is highlighted by the example of a forces commander who comprehensively beats better-equipped opposition in a US military exercise because he consistently does the opposite of what the computers predict.
- He goes on to show that, strangely, it is possible to give 'structure' to spontaneity, by consciously going against the grain in order to generate an outcome that is surprising to the other party, but not to you.

What you have to watch

- Although the subject matter is fascinating, there are so many experts interviewed that the average reader would not be able to enact any of the skills necessary to take advantage of the findings, other than the basic point that you should trust your first instincts more.

How could this thinking be applied to your business?

Simply Brilliant, Fergus O'Connell

What the book says

- The best ideas aren't always complicated and the incredibly straightforward stuff is often overlooked in the search for a complex answer.
- Many smart people lack the set of essential skills which could roughly be described as 'common sense'.

- There are seven principles here that can be adapted for attacking most everyday problems
  1. Many things are simple – *despite our tendency to complicate them.*
  2. You need to know what you're trying to do – *many don't.*
  3. There is always a sequence of events – *make the journey in your head.*
  4. Things don't get done if people don't do them – *strategic wafflers beware!*
  5. Things rarely turn out as expected – *so plan for the unexpected.*
  6. Things either are or they aren't – *don't fudge things.*
  7. Look at things from other's point of view – *it will help your expectations.*

What's good about it

- In a world of over complication, asking some simple questions can really make your life easier. For example:
  - What would be the simplest thing to do here?
  - Describing an issue or a solution in less than 25 words.
  - Telling it as though you were telling a six year old.
  - Asking whether there is a simpler way.
- Try writing the minutes of a meeting before the meeting – then you'll know what you want to get out of it.
- It highlights the difference between duration and effort. *'How long will it take you to have a look at that?' 'About an hour.'* But when?
- It explains the reasons why things don't get done: confusion, over-commitment, inability – usually busy people never say there's a problem!
- Plan your time assuming you will have interruptions – the *'hot date'* scenario.

What you have to watch

- The orientation is very much based on a project management perspective, which is fine if you are one, but others may prefer to cherry-pick the most applicable ideas.
- Anyone who flies by the seat of their pants would have to be very disciplined to apply these ideas. It's a bit like dieting.

How could this thinking be applied to your business?

Appendix 3: The full survey

The questionnaire

I have been commissioned to write a book called *Teach Yourself Growing Your Business,* and I am asking for your help. If you have the time, could you possibly answer any of the six questions below? I am soliciting opinion from those I know that have run businesses, large and small, and I hope to use some of the material in the book. If you reply, I will assume that you don't mind being quoted, but if you would prefer not, please tell me.

The questions

1 What is the hardest thing about growing your business?
2 Is growth always a good thing?
3 Did you ever suffer from post-launch blues or a three-year itch?
4 How do you plan the 'next big thing'?
5 If you could have known one thing when you started that you know now, what would it be?
6 Is there anything else you would like to pass on about growing or evolving your business?

Groupings by company size

- Sole trader
- Small partnerships (two or three people)
- Fewer than 10 staff
- 10–50 staff
- More than 50 staff

The responses

Sole traders

ROBERT ASHTON, Author and entrepreneur

What is the hardest thing about growing your business?
Staying focused.

Is growth always a good thing?
No – being true to yourself and your ideals is better.

Did you ever suffer from post-launch blues or a three-year itch?
Yes, but at seven years. I sold up both times.

How do you plan the 'next big thing'?
Listen, look, think and make notes.

If you could have known one thing when you started that you know now, what would it be?
It's tough as hell but worth the struggle.

Is there anything else you'd like to pass on about growing or evolving your business?
Well, I'd naturally like your readers to buy my book – but your editor might not approve!

MELANIE RYDER, Copywriter and communications consultant

What is the hardest thing about growing your business?

1 Taking the leap in the first place. Exiting the comfort zone of conventional salaries. Entering the world of answering to yourself and knowing when to self-praise instead of knocking yourself. Bouncing things off walls, rather than colleagues. The lack of any instruction whatsoever – even packets of tomato seeds come with a picture!

2 Managing the period where initial panic and excitement gives way to practicality and, invariably, reality (including setbacks). Knowing the difference between taking on more of the same and taking on something that heralds progress. Understanding that, when it's quite possible to work 24/7 and still have work left over you MUST switch off and enjoy yourself. Learning from your contemporaries, but distinguishing between what's working for them, and what isn't. Understanding that compromising your opinions needn't constitute compromising your standards. Being selfish when you're normally a nice person. Recognizing that your own success will attract the right, and more often the wrong, kind of people, for both reasons. Not being walked over. At the same time, not being paranoid.

Is growth always a good thing?
It can be brilliant. It can also be fatal. I suppose it really depends on what you set out to achieve in the first place. If it's pound signs and you're prepared to bend over and be shafted then, if

you're lucky, growth is great. If your motives are to walk away from corporate politics and creative compromise, then growth could plonk you back where you came from, unless you're careful.

How do you plan the 'next big thing'?
Intuitively, but then again I'm quite lucky because I can do more than one of the roles involved in my industry, so I can change hats. How do you plan the 'next big thing?' I guess you look at whatever trusted sources are saying the 'next big thing' will be in your industry and either do the same, better, or do the complete opposite, memorably. I don't plan so I can't answer most of that question.

If you could have known one thing when you started that you know now, what would it be?
That I could actually do it. That, knowing that I could actually do it, that I actually would – one day – do it. And to that end enjoying the job(s) I hated previously a little more, and using my time there to forge a more structured future self-employment plan of attack.

Is there anything else you'd like to pass on about growing or evolving your business?
The worst thing you can do in life is look back and wonder 'what if'. Provided you can eat, and have a good mate that can put you up if you have to go into liquidation, take the leap. Every single business in the entire history of the universe began with one thing: possibility.

MARK TURNER, Agent and music publisher

What is the hardest thing about growing your business?
The lack of hours in a day.

Is growth always a good thing?
Growth has many forms. One could call reducing company staff and company expenses growth, if the company were to have a better bottom line figure. Sometimes growth can be time spent learning not to make the same mistakes.

Did you ever suffer from post-launch blues or a three-year itch?
Yes! We live in, and are part of, a society that forever wants more. Our dreams and wants are continually expanding. On a personal note, I've been building a new company website and in writing out where the company is right now, I realized I've already clearly surpassed all my initial expectations, but hey, my

initial expectations aren't what I want now. Itchy times in a company are good, as it makes you continually reassess.

How do you plan the 'next big thing'?

Planning for the next big thing is the easy part. The next big thing has to start life as a creative idea. I make sure I'm always tuned into what's happening around me, and set aside time to think outside the box. Usually an idea comes to me when talking to people and hearing about their lives.

If you could have known one thing when you started that you know now, what would it be?

Listen to your gut feeling, as it's usually right.

Is there anything else you'd like to pass on about growing or evolving your business?

You have to love what you do. Let me say that again: YOU HAVE TO LOVE WHAT YOU DO. Basically, everyone is selling something, and if you can't get excited about what you're selling, how will the client? Be patient and be ready to act when the right opportunities/ideas present themselves. Always have a forward plan to work to. Writing forward plans/lists is time well spent. Within growing any business, people skills are paramount. Develop 100 per cent faith and persistence.

KATRINE BIRK, Research analyst

What is the hardest thing about growing your business?

The hardest part is to keep motivation high as it is easy to slip into a routine. Brainstorming new ideas is difficult in a one-man band, unless you deliberately seek out new learning, best practice and inspirations from proven business sources.

Is growth always a good thing?

Growth is always a good thing if it is what you planned for. If you don't have a contingency plan in place for sudden expansion opportunities, the way you handle growth could be your downfall. Luckily, small businesses in the UK have the opportunity to tap into a great network of contacts making it much easier to pull in skills and support needed to deal effectively and professionally with growth when your company is not quite aligned to deal with the extra commitment.

Did you ever suffer from post-launch blues or a three-year itch?

Yes. Sometimes overwhelmed by the extent of things to manage, other times depressed by the lack of business. But all in all, nothing a bit of mental rationalizing won't take care of.

How do you plan the 'next big thing'?

Always scan business press for openings, opportunities and ideas. These leads provide a base for unique initiatives projecting a more customized approach. Being on the receiving end, one thing I hate is a mass-produced mailing for example.

If you could have known one thing when you started that you know now, what would it be?

A greater understanding of the selling points which best trigger an income-generating response. And being more confident about it.

DAF JONES, Session musician

What is the hardest thing about growing your business?

Gaining, developing and maintaining those important and useful contacts.

Is growth always a good thing?

Yes, as long as quality of service is maintained.

Did you ever suffer from post-launch blues or a three-year itch?

Yes. Life as a professional musician can be a rollercoaster ride at the best of times.

How do you plan the 'next big thing'?

By doing my homework.

If you could have known one thing when you started that you know now, what would it be?

Networking is essential as talent alone in some cases is not enough.

Is there anything else you'd like to pass on about growing or evolving your business?

If you really believe in yourself, and in what you want to achieve, you owe it to yourself to give it a go, regardless of any negative outside opinion.

JOHN OWRID, Marketing specialist

What is the hardest thing about growing your business?

Patience.

Is growth always a good thing?

No, there's good growth and bad growth. In the early days bad growth is doing things for money when you should be doing it for your reputation.

Did you ever suffer from post-launch blues or a three-year itch?
Yes – it's horrible.

How do you plan the 'next big thing'?
On day one – you'll never get round to it otherwise.

If you could have known one thing when you started that you know now, what would it be?
To know which 50 per cent of the clichés about starting businesses were true.

Is there anything else you'd like to pass on about growing or evolving your business?
Stick with it – starting a business is like batting like Boycott (boring, unglamorous, yet remarkably rewarding for brute perseverance).

IAN FARROW, Communications adviser

What is the hardest thing about growing your business?
Deciding how much control to cede. I'm still in the early stages of setting up a new business but I'm already facing tough decisions about growth. The hardest decision for me is how much control to cede in my new company in the pursuit of growth through partnership working. I have been approached by a much larger brand in my sector to form a partnership and must negotiate cannily to maintain my independence and build my fledgling brand.

Is growth always a good thing?
I have always read that growing quicker than the capacity the business can handle can be catastrophic because cash flow and production problems scupper any future benefit. However, I also think growth can take you off course. I think you need to bear in mind what you started the business for and make sure you grow in that direction.

Did you ever suffer from post-launch blues or a three-year itch?
Being still new to the world of the entrepreneur I have yet to itch. However, my first promotional activity gave me a huge confidence problem. You tend to forget that your business is not as important to your prospects as it is to you. Your new venture is like a new child – you want everyone to say it's a beauty. If the response is anything less, then the resulting post-natal depression can make you take your eye off what's important. I also think it only natural that there is a low after a launch as your focus becomes more rational. You need to see a launch

very much as the beginning of the beginning rather than the end of the beginning.

How do you plan the 'next big thing'?

I think it's important to keep your big picture clear and at the forefront of everything you do. Opportunities will come that require quick decisions that could influence the direction of your growth. For me it's imperative that these are not lost but nor do they set me on a different course from the one on which I started. Basically, be flexible about how you get there but not about where you're going.

If you could have known one thing when you started that you know now, what would it be?

A clearer picture of my worth in the marketplace.

Is there anything else you'd like to pass on about growing or evolving your business?

I'm still a minnow; ask me when I'm a pike.

PETER GAZE, Public affairs adviser

What is the hardest thing about growing your business?

In the early stages, there is a great deal of unused time. Much of the problem is boredom, which can be demoralizing. The key is using that time effectively to secure new business and to banish guilt. If you cannot contribute to your new business effort with an additional hour's work then take the kids to a museum or go for a walk – it will be better for you in the long run.

Is growth always a good thing?

Revenue and profit growth is always a good thing. Bowing to clients' pressure to take on staff/additional staff is something that needs to be thought about extremely carefully. It's important to have a clear understanding of how much money one wants to extract from the business over a certain time period. It may be that staying as small as possible may achieve that net profit goal whereas staff growth may destroy it completely.

Did you ever suffer from post-launch blues or a three-year itch?

Personally no, but those around you who love you most will suffer because they care about you deeply but for very good reasons you have to keep them a certain distance from developments. Do not let them ride the emotional rollercoaster with you, however often and strenuously they plead.

How do you plan the 'next big thing'?
Next big things insert themselves into my brain continually. I deal with them by talking them through with respected individuals (including clients) who talk me out of them – they know I'm onto a good thing.

If you could have known one thing when you started that you know now, what would it be?
Difficult, very difficult, to answer. I would like to say that I wish I'd known how long it was going to take to get it off the ground (two years). However, had I known that and articulated it to those who have supported me, I might not have done it. Catch 22.

Is there anything else you'd like to pass on about growing or evolving your business?
Take all reasonable steps to prevent business leaving but do not get hung up on it. In consultancy, if it wants to go, let it go and remember it fondly. The important thing is to keep it coming in through the front door.

TIM LAWLER, Creative communications writer

What is the hardest thing about growing your business?
Keeping motivated. If you have no problems with inclination, and are convinced that your commercial pursuit is the best thing you could be doing with your life (rather than, say, taking the kids swimming more or spending a day a week on the novel/photography course/etc.) – and that having more of whatever it brings would definitely be worth the effort – then you'll find the time to make those calls, put in the strategic thinking time, pitch that extension to your usual remit. If not, it will appear that the hardest thing is finding the time, but that will be nonsense. Unless you never ever watch TV or go out, in which case see next answer.

Is growth always a good thing?
Absolutely not. Keeping up with inflation is good, any more is optional. There's a lot to be said for ticking over and sleeping well.

Did you ever suffer from post-launch blues or a three-year itch?
Three-month! No but seriously. It has to keep transforming into a shinier, newer version of itself, which mine tends to do every nine months or so. Then I have a rubbish three months and then something positive happens, apparently out of the blue but

there's no such thing as pure luck, and I'm back in the saddle again.

How do you plan the 'next big thing'?

It comes to me. Sometimes figuratively, sometimes literally, like a phone call. If it ever didn't, I'd go for a long walk and then it would.

If you could have known one thing when you started that you know now, what would it be?

No one's as surprised by your fees as you are – but repeat business still has its price-elasticity limits. Staying gung-ho on price is one way to appear good at what you do, but it doesn't work like that in all disciplines. People often perceive they can buy what you sell from a cheaper source – especially copywriting. The trick is keeping them reminded of why you're worth it.

Is there anything else you'd like to pass on about growing or evolving your business?

Setting deadlines is good. Hunger is useful. Greed is usually transparent. You're probably better than you think you are. There are some people it's just not worth trying with. I could go on.

MARCEL FEIGEL, Freelance copywriter

What is the hardest thing about growing your business?

Maintaining control. I find that growth comes in funny spurts, with a few steps back along the way. While we may have an idea or even a plan, of how we would like to see our business grow, my experience is that it doesn't usually happen that way.

Is growth always a good thing?

Too much quick growth, which is what most companies want, can definitely be a bad thing because it's easy to lose your identity or working ethos along the way. When you grow too quickly you have to rush things through, sometimes need to employ extra staff without having enough time to carefully go through all the applicants and choose the best people. As a result you can lose direction and see all your early ideals fall by the wayside. That's where blindly pursuing profit can become a liability.

Did you ever suffer from post-launch blues or a three-year itch?

I don't know about the three-year itch, but I can testify to the post-launch blues. Once the honeymoon period is over, and you get over the excitement of having your own business, you realize that you're working harder than you were before and sometimes for less than you were earning before. Which definitely leaves you blue.

How do you plan the 'next big thing'?
First, by gauging how I'm currently doing, then seeing what is currently happening in the business. I then try and assess how what I do can best fit in with the prevailing climate. Do I need to zag, or is it better to zig?

If you could have known one thing when you started that you know now, what would it be?
Just how much work, and how much incidental work, I would be involved in. When I started I thought it would be a simple matter of going after projects and then executing them. As a sole operator it's easy to think that way. But what I learned the hard way is that doing the actual work is often the easiest part. Obtaining the work and then getting paid for it are often the most difficult and the most time-consuming parts.

Is there anything else you'd like to pass on about growing or evolving your business?
In line with the previous question, I would say it is important to remember that you are a business, you are a company and that is the way you must think of yourself.

SUE BUCKLE, Career and personal development coach

What is the hardest thing about growing your business?
Not sure I have actually grown my business, nor did I/do I want to ... I just wanted independence and autonomy.

Is growth always a good thing?
I don't think so. It can be at the expense of quality and personal service. I particularly don't think every business should go public. I've learned that 'mergers' are always 'takeovers' and result in people being made redundant and miserable.

Did you ever suffer from post-launch blues or a three-year itch?
Yes, it is lonely and scary having to do everything by yourself, and if things get difficult, there is only one person to sort them out. On the other hand, I have an understanding, lovely boss!!!

How do you plan the next big thing?
I haven't. Coaching has evolved from recruitment, and I'm not even thinking about what happens next.

If you could have known one thing when you started that you know now, what would it be?

How you can't and mustn't take rejection personally.

STEPHEN MARTIN, Customer analyst

What is the hardest thing about growing your business?

Maintaining momentum. Just when you have worked your tail off on a big project you still have to pick yourself up and keep selling. Sales is okay provided you make the contacts but keeping at the contacting is hard work.

Is growth always a good thing?

No, especially not when it is hard to maintain quality and also personal interest and fun. I set up business to have some fun earning a living and sometimes growth can drive the fun out.

Did you ever suffer from post-launch blues or a three-year itch?

Having set up businesses three times I have always found year two the hardest. Year one you have newness and old contacts on your side, by year two you have run out of these and need to find the behaviour suitable for an ongoing business. If you haven't fixed it by year three you are dead.

How do you plan the 'next big thing'?

Good question – still working on that! But holidays are a good time for reflection and I always come back with more ideas.

If you could have known one thing when you started that you know now, what would it be?

Marketing/sales/networking seldom works in a way you predict but if you do nothing then you get nothing. The best form of marketing is to have a simple sentence that describes what you do so that people can remember and pass on your description. Your business is much better when other people are doing the selling on your behalf.

Is there anything else you'd like to pass on about growing or evolving your business?

Decide how you will measure your success and keep track of it. If your measure is three months' holiday a year or attending all your children's school events or making £1 million, it is all valid but you need to find a measure that fits you. If you don't know where you are going you will never know when you have arrived.

CAROL DUKES, Media consultant

What is the hardest thing about growing your business?
Making new sales and developing the product at the same time as servicing the growing base of existing clients, suppliers etc. Finding the time and energy for recruitment and then training of new staff – it's hard to take the financial risk of hiring ahead of the curve but it's very easy then to find yourself 'too busy to delegate'.

Is growth always a good thing?
Depends why you set up in business in the first place. If you want to become wealthy beyond your wildest dreams then growth is probably at least usually good, so long as it's profitable. If, however, you are more interested in autonomy or creativity or some non-financial measure then growth could be your worst enemy – at some point you will be spending all your time managing staff and/or investors rather than engaging in your chosen business.

Did you ever suffer from post-launch blues or a three-year itch?
Yes – I think this is very common because entrepreneurs are often good 'starters' or 'creators' but poor at routine.

How do you plan the 'next big thing'?
I don't think you can – it's like falling in love and you can't plan that. However there are times in your life when you are likely to be susceptible, and then it's a matter of being very open to new ideas, staying well-informed and making unlikely connections.

If you could have known one thing when you started that you know now, what would it be?
Equity is forever. Be very careful about who you cut in on an equity basis as it will be very hard or expensive to extricate them further down the track. Profit share generally achieves a lot of the same incentivization, particularly when your shares aren't publicly traded.

Is there anything else you'd like to pass on about growing or evolving your business?
Read Kevin Duncan's books!

ANTHONY PRICE, Business and legal consultant

What is the hardest thing about growing your business?
Converting interest into income.

Is growth always a good thing?
No, but I'd generally prefer to be troubled by excessive growth than none at all.

Did you ever suffer from post-launch blues or a three-year itch?
Definitely had post-launch blues, but can't comment on a three-year itch.

How do you plan the 'next big thing'?
Find time to step back from the detail work, and someone you trust to talk to.

If you could have known one thing when you started that you know now, what would it be?
That two years later I'd be back in employment again.

Is there anything else you'd like to pass on about growing or evolving your business?
Never underestimate the value of talking to people about it. Anyone, everyone. And make sure you enjoy the process of building the business, not just the dream of what you will one day achieve.

NICK MIDDLETON, TV presenter, author, academic tutor

What is the hardest thing about growing your business?
Increasing the price tag of my outputs (while not wanting to increase the number of employees from 1 to 1+).

Is growth always a good thing?
Certainly not. Too many people are too obsessed with growth as a mantra. Your next book should be called 'Teach Yourself Evolving your Business'. Greater profit always sounds nice but at what cost in other departments? Remember the difference between price and value.

Did you ever suffer from post-launch blues or a three-year itch?
No.

How do you plan the 'next big thing'?
With a lot of careful thought and by talking to people who know more about it than I do.

If you could have known one thing when you started that you know now, what would it be?
Working on your own can be a lonesome business. This is compounded by the attitude of many others (who don't work

for themselves) who often view the self-employed as being semi-retired people working only when they feel like it. Being your own boss does allow you to be flexible, but in my experience it can also often mean working harder because no one else will do it for you and if you don't do it, you don't get paid.

DAVE BENNETT, Print consultant

I would revert to The Five Ps: Proper Planning Prevents Poor Performance.

The only bad decision is no decision (you can always change your mind at a later date).

Do not listen to the dissenters, the world is full of negative people and in the words of that global giant we all love to hate – Just do it ...

Small partnerships (two or three people)

STEVE GREENSTED, Two-person marketing consultancy

What is the hardest thing about growing your business?
Finding the right balance between going after new business and smothering your existing clients in love and attention.

Is growth always a good thing?
Yes. Clients come and go. Your business is a leaky bucket, which needs to be topped up constantly. You have to be careful to manage your growth though, or, perversely, it might bankrupt you.

Did you ever suffer from post-launch blues or a three-year itch?
We've only been going two years, so I'm still thoroughly enjoying the novelty of working for myself.

How do you plan the 'next big thing'?
We're not planning the next big thing. In addition to general business and marketing consultancy, we now do headhunting as well as M&A, but neither were planned. We're merely doing what our clients seem to want us to do even if we didn't set out to do either of these. Providing we know what we're doing, enjoy it and make money out of it, that's fine. One of my bosses said to me years ago that there are only three bases for taking on a client:

1 They'll buy great work from you.
2 You'll have fun.
3 You'll make money.

Any two will do.

If you could have known one thing when you started that you know now, what would it be?
I sort of knew it. And wasn't wrong. Things never happen as quickly as you want and need.

Is there anything else you'd like to pass on about growing or evolving your business?
Yes. When you make a phone call, write a letter, attend a meeting or do a pitch, there are only three possible outcomes. The client, potential or current, is either going to like it, loathe it, or be undecided. None of these are personal, so be brave, say what you really think, and go to bed knowing you did your best.

HELEN ASCOTT, Two-person design partnership

What is the hardest thing about growing your business?
Taking a risk, trusting that your judgment and abilities will sustain any growth.

If you could have known one thing when you started that you know now, what would it be?
That potential clients lie, and however ethically you may run your business the waters are still shark infested. Cynical and naive at the same time maybe, but a tough lesson to learn.

NIK DONE, Two-person public relations consultancy

What is the hardest thing about growing your business?
In our case it's been working around all the legal restrictions which have been tough due to restrictive covenants.

Is growth always a good thing?
You have to weigh up what's most important: a) a higher turnover with more business which is likely to help attract more clients and good employees but might be less profitable and harder to manage if achieved too soon; or b) a tighter ship with better margins and therefore profit, but which looks, initially, less impressive. This is one of our year one challenges.

Did you ever suffer from post-launch blues or a three-year itch?

Yup – after about a month. We had client number one but number two was very hard to get. It can be very demoralizing – as can working semi on your own when you've always been used to a big team within a lively environment. Creating a more structured environment and giving myself credit for what I'd already achieved really helped.

How do you plan the 'next big thing'?

Too busy dealing with this one right now!

If you could have known one thing when you started that you know now, what would it be?

Taking the pressure off by realizing that you've got enough cash in the bank to feed your family for a year because it's really not going to be all that simple!

HELEN EDWARDS, Specialist travel agency, one partner, one staff

What is the hardest thing about growing your business?

Taking the plunge, anxiety about the consequences: risk, responsibility, staff, salaries, technology and financing it all ...

Is growth always a good thing?

Not sure ... but the reason for our hesitancy in going ahead with it is doubtless because deep down we believe indeed it is not!

Did you ever suffer from post-launch blues or a three-year itch?

No, can honestly say we didn't. Every year new accounts have come on board and after three years we moved to new offices, which was new and exciting.

How do you plan the 'next big thing'?

By costing it accurately with realistic financial forecasts, ensuring like-minded people are brought in to support the growth, as we are in a very niche area of our business, and attention to detail really matters, and a company name to live up to.

If you could have known one thing when you started that you know now, what would it be?

If we knew what we know now before we started we would have done it earlier! The business has evolved relatively smoothly and new business has come our way as our reputation has grown, which has been rewarding. We have never really had to pitch hard for new accounts. Conversely, until quite recently we have never considered growing the business and actively seeking more lucrative accounts.

Is there anything else you'd like to pass on about growing or evolving your business?

We started as a partnership six-and-a-half years ago (and later became a limited company) and after three years employed one part-time assistant who is now full-time. To be honest at the outset it was never about making serious money but has given us – the two directors – a comfortable income. The position we are in now is that one or other of us may want to step aside in a few years and at this stage the company is not 'worth anything' unless we grow it. We have come to realize that we'd like some reward at the end of, say, ten years. We would need to employ account managers that our client hotels are totally comfortable with. Currently the company is simply the reputation of the two of us in the trade. And the travel industry is renowned for low, low margins and expectations are high for very low returns. We are trying to change this image and provide better services to show that higher fees are justified and in the long run make sense. So for others setting up or growing, don't sell yourselves too cheap, don't be afraid to move on from something if it is not working – we have resigned accounts but never lost one and if we feel uncomfortable with someone or with falling standards, we move one.

NICLAS LJUNGBERG, Brand strategist, three-person partnership

What is the hardest thing about growing your business?

Moving from working with clients you want to work with to being stuck with selling the organization you have to sustain cash flow.

Is growth always a good thing?

No, for the above reason. Then again if you don't grow you're stuck selling the one service or product that you or a very small team can deliver.

Did you ever suffer from post-launch blues or a three-year itch?

Post-launch definitely, in that as the company evolves you realize that you and your partners have to evolve along with it and change mindsets about lots of things from operations to strategy.

If you could have known one thing when you started that you know now, what would it be?

If you get into business with other people in any kind of shared ownership be crystal clear on who you think your clients are, what you think your service or product is and what it does for your customers, how that is going to be delivered and by whom, and exactly what each of you bring to, and take out of, the business.

Is there anything else you would like to pass on about growing or evolving your business?

Nah. Go make the mistakes and learn.

JULIAN DAVIES, Finance consultant, three-person partnership

What is the hardest thing about growing your business?

Bringing in the additional revenue that creates growth. Managing growth is not easy but generating the extra sales and profit is the hardest part. To be able to do this successfully you need a good market positioning, good marketing, good selling technique and good negotiating – you obviously then need to deliver the good/services consistently at a high quality level.

Is growth always a good thing?

I do not think growth should be for growth's sake. Growth should mean bigger profits (more than enough to justify the extra hassle that growth brings) and not just size.

Did you ever suffer from post-launch blues or a three-year itch?

Yes, it's not all a bed of roses; there are highs and lows in business, you have to be able to deal with them both.

How do you plan the 'next big thing'?

I don't think you can formally plan for the next big thing. However you must be prepared to chat to many different types of people in different markets and trades to hear lots of ideas and get a feel for possible trends. You then have to be prepared to have a punt on something you feel may succeed even if others don't agree.

If you could have known one thing when you started that you know now, what would it be?

Firstly how tough it can be sometimes and secondly that it is the same for everyone else in business. It's easy to get down when things don't go as planned and easy to take it personally when it is your own business. I wish I had been told that everyone running and growing a business goes through some big lows, that is when you need to keep motivated and positive and keep going.

Is there anything else you'd like to pass on about growing or evolving your business?

You can't possibly know everything, talk to as many people as possible in the same or different industries and also to people with varied experience. Business is not a science but an art, you need to be able to adapt to different situations, a combination of yours and other people's experience will help you do that well.

GERRY HOPKINSON, Two-person public relations consultancy

What is the hardest thing about growing your business?

The hardest thing about growing your business is letting go and involving other people – collaboration is the key to success.

Is growth always a good thing?

Yes. It may not always be comfortable, but it's better than the alternative. If businesses don't grow they die, or grow stagnant. Growth is vital for business and it's up to each business to manage the challenge it represents.

Did you ever suffer from post-launch blues or a three-year itch?

No, but then I've never been one to be depressed.

How do you plan the 'next big thing'?

You don't. All you can do is be aware of what's going on around you and develop antennae that let you pick up things earlier than everyone else. You only need to be five minutes ahead of the pack to succeed, in fact if you're too far ahead you'll probably fail.

If you could have known one thing when you started that you know now, what would it be?

All businesses are people businesses. Invest in friendships and relationships and the rest will happen quite naturally.

Is there anything else you'd like to pass on about growing or evolving your business?

Businesses evolve, and the best ones are rarely the same now as when they started out – so embrace change and accept that the important thing is to stay in business and grow. The rest is secondary.

IRMA HAMILTON-HUNT, Recruitment consultant

What is the hardest thing about growing your business?
The hardest thing about growing your business is keeping yourself motivated. I have set up a couple of businesses from scratch and the first one was a lot easier as I had a brilliant business partner and we motivated each other.

Is growth always a good thing?
I now believe that growth is not necessarily a good thing as I found that I made more money in recruitment when I had fewer staff and smaller offices and I was more in control.

Did you ever suffer from post-launch blues or a three-year itch?
Not really a three-year itch but I did always know either when it was time to move on or diversify.

Is there anything else you would like to pass on about growing or evolving your business?
Two things: always know your business partner inside out, and don't forget that you have to pay tax on everything you earn.

Fewer than 10 staff

DAMIAN CLARKSON, Founder, event management company, 7 staff

What is the hardest thing about growing your business?
Finding the team to share your vision and deliver to your standards.

Is growth always a good thing?
No. We do not aim to be large and available. Rapid growth endangers quality and reputation. Safe growth keeps your clients as advocates. Our objective is never to have more than ten staff.

Did you ever suffer from post-launch blues or a three-year itch?
We get involved with planning special memorable occasions such as weddings and it's very exciting and privileged. I have received many texts from brides on honeymoon!

How do you plan the 'next big thing'?
Consensually, with the team. I can't deliver this myself.

If you could have known one thing when you started that you know now, what would it be?
Competitors are just that. They will kill for your business.

Is there anything else you'd like to pass on about growing or evolving your business?
Reputation in any market is worth more than anything else.

GUS WILLIAMS, Owner, marketing agency, 9 staff

What is the hardest thing about growing your business?
Maintaining a focus on new business whilst delivering high quality work to existing customers – especially when you are busy and expanding 'organically' within your existing customer base. Oh, yes, and getting the timing right when expanding capacity.

Is growth always a good thing?
Not necessarily. Controlled and planned growth is, but knowing when to turn down business is an important lesson to learn.

Did you ever suffer from post-launch blues or a three-year itch?
No, but you do need to take holidays and switch the phone off.

How do you plan the 'next big thing'?
Just get on with it, keep lifting your head up and be ready to take opportunities.

If you could have known one thing when you started that you know now, what would it be?
To keep cool and remember that running your own business is, and will always be, a rollercoaster ride, try to enjoy the ups and not get too uptight about the downs.

Is there anything else you'd like to pass on about growing or evolving your business?
Your family is more important than anything else, don't exclude them from what's going on, you'll need them for the ups as well as the downs.

Oh, yes, and never lend anyone your bike.

You can quote me if you like but I want a picture, inside back cover, on a fire escape, looking up, moody, black & white ...

ADAM SUNDERLAND, Founder, outsourced marketing agency, 4 staff

What is the hardest thing about growing your business?
The single largest challenge is overcoming the 'Nobody ever got fired for hiring IBM' phenomenon. Customers embrace the notion of change, but when faced with taking the radical step of

doing something new and different, risk aversion creeps in. As a consequence, the second largest challenge becomes finding customers brave enough to act upon their disillusionment or disappointment with the status quo, and to do something about it.

Is growth always a good thing?

Growth is never a good thing – it's either a great thing or a disastrous thing. If growth is properly managed and does not compromise what you set out to achieve in the first place, great! If it is properly managed and you can live with the consequences of change to what you set out to achieve in the first place, great again. But if growth is not properly managed and/or you are uncomfortable with the changes you need to make to accommodate growth, then chances are things are going to go horribly wrong. Somewhere here there is a tie to the famous Bill Bernbach quote of 'A principle isn't a principle until it costs you money'. That said, there are two things that are worse than growth – standing still and, worse, going backwards.

Did you ever suffer from post-launch blues or a three-year itch?

Is the Pope Catholic? Does a monk take a drink now and then? I can't believe that anyone would ever answer 'No' to this – or if they do, that they're telling the truth. Once the immediacy of launch is over, the feeling is similar to that of having completed a new business pitch – an immediate high followed by a lowness until the next high comes along. You cannot be on a high 100 percent of the time – at least not legally – and hence there is always going to be a period of 'bluesiness' that follows. As regards the 'three-year itch', can I get back to you in two-and-a-half years?

How do you plan the 'next big thing'?

With a great deal of luck as well as pluck.

If you could have known one thing when you started that you know now, what would it be?

However hard you think it is to take the plunge, it's only the beginning and there's a whole lot more hardship to follow. That's not to say it's not fun, just make sure you're prepared for the rollercoaster ride you're going to take, and recognize that there's no longer a choice between 'work to live' or 'live to work' as the divide between personal life and work to all intents disappears.

Is there anything else you'd like to pass on about growing or evolving your business?

At some stage in your life, go for your own business – it may not suit you and you may end up back in the corporate world, but equally you may find that you love being master of your own destiny – and it would be a hell of a shame to look back one day and regret that you'd never tested your mettle.

DENISE HAIRE, Partner, TV production company, 4 staff

What is the hardest thing about growing your business?

For me, I have a huge desire to not only keep our overheads to a minimum, and also not to have the responsibility of staff to think about. Luckily, we are in a business whereby we can employ people on a job-for-job basis, which means their fees are covered.

Is growth always a good thing?

I think growth can be a good thing, and perhaps done in stepping stones, and closely monitored and managed to ensure productivity and not waste occurring.

Did you ever suffer from post-launch blues or a three-year itch?

Yes and yes.

How do you plan the 'next big thing'?

My plan is to get us all to plan and for us, that is a big thing – beginning with weekly meetings.

If you could have known one thing when you started that you know now, what would it be?

Make sure you like what you are doing and be with the people you enjoy being with.

KAREN BROOKS, Owner, public relations agency, 3 staff

What is the hardest thing about growing your business?

I don't want my business to get too big – I had severe cash flow problems years ago. The tricky thing is finding the balance – approaching new clients to maintain the client/income level in balance, without over-stretching yourself both in terms of staffing and outgoings. I try to find a level where we give new and current clients the attention they need, whilst keeping an ear to the ground for new opportunities in case one project terminates suddenly or a client goes under.

Is growth always a good thing?

As far as I am concerned growth is not always a good thing. I started my own business because I enjoy what I do – I love the fact that if it's a sunny day I can let the staff go early on a Friday or have my god-daughter over to play at working, without upsetting anyone. If the business got too big you get into all sorts of 'political' situations – staffing, training, more dealings with my bank manager – I'd be running a company not doing work I enjoy.

Did you ever suffer from post-launch blues or a three-year itch?

When everything went wrong a few years ago I did question what I was doing and if I should go and do something else – but this presents so many challenges and starting all over again was the biggest. I'm lucky no day is ever the same and as I'm my own boss if I decide to take the company in a slightly different direction we do – it stops the boredom setting in.

How do you plan the 'next big thing'?

I have always found that if you plan the Next Big Thing – it never really works out the way you expect – so I have a somewhat fluid approach to it – I have an idea where I want to go but am always open to other opportunities too. If you are too tunnel vision about where you want to go you can miss out on some other great things.

If you could have known one thing when you started that you know now, what would it be?

Get a good bookkeeper and chase those invoices!

Is there anything else you'd like to pass on about growing or evolving your business?

Get a good bookkeeper and chase those invoices!

DOMINIC ARMSTRONG, Founder, recruitment company, 3 staff

What is the hardest thing about growing your business?

I think it is the realization that, whilst you obviously need to work ON the business (in terms of strategy, marketing, PR and overall direction etc.) you really do need to remember to also work IN your business. Personally I was too focused on wanting to 'create' the entity and, through personal pride or ego, thought that the company was going to change the world! In reality, I think that I forgot the real reason I set up the company in the first place (apart from the work–life balance) which was that people were buying ME for my experience and expertise.

Is growth always a good thing?

I always used to think it was the ONLY objective. Now, however, I have come to recognize that it is probably not always a good thing. You cannot be all things to all people – if you set up your business because people wanted to buy you, then there is a chance that if you grow you spread yourself too thin – and end up 'passing the buck' or delegating roles or responsibility to others, which negates the personal effect.

Did you ever suffer from post-launch blues or a three-year itch?

Not post-launch – more euphoria and excitement that I was about to conquer or change the world! Three years definitely! I think in year one you work all hours establishing the business knowing that is what is needed. At year end you've made a modest turnover and hopefully have made profit, although you don't really mind because you are so excited that you CAN do it and have done it!

Year two you start to see the business grow and towards the end of the year you realize that things are going well. Subconsciously you start to take your foot of the gas. Year end and you've doubled turnover and doubled profitability. You are so excited because you've proved you have done it!

Year three, you coast, you cruise, you enjoy the success, you delegate, you concentrate ON the business, you dream of expanding, you think big picture. You forget to work IN the business. Deals don't go according to plan – you miss a few easy wins because you've overlooked the detail and forgotten to go back to basics. Cash flow worries start to crop up and then, before you know where you are, you hit the wall. There is a sudden realization that you've got to act and act fast otherwise it could all go horribly wrong. The sleepless nights worrying about paying the staff start. You question why on earth you started in the first place. Your friends see how worried you look and suggest you can close the business and go and get a proper job – any job – just to pay the mortgage. You cut back expenses, culling anything that isn't essential. You get back on the phone and TALK to people because you suddenly remember that all the PR and fancy marketing ideas are NO substitute for actually talking to the people that bought YOU in the first place.

How do you plan the 'next big thing'?

In terms of product, I tend to listen to the market, watch the competition, listen to my clients, then act. I also try to anticipate what issue or trend is going to impact my market – e.g. I ran a survey last year on employment screening in London hotels to clarify in my own mind that I thought hotels were not being proactive enough in screening employees. Results showed that they didn't carry effective screening. I then approached a security screening company with findings and started to create a product focused on the hotels' needs. This year after countless focus groups and tests we launched the product.

If you could have known one thing when you started that you know now, what would it be?
Keep it simple and get the basics right.

Is there anything else you'd like to pass on about growing or evolving your business?
I think that my three-year itch analogy adequately sums up my own experiences.

ANDREW WHITE, Owner, public relations agency, 3 staff

What is the hardest thing about growing your business?
The hardest thing is taking the decision to grow and be responsible for the costs of people/plant and premises. Working for yourself you can pretty much take the salary that you want, but when you take on a team, you have to make sure that they come first, that they are paid first, motivated, that they take their holidays. By taking the decision to grow, make sure you have right team around you to facilitate the growth and that they come up to your expectations.

Is growth always a good thing?
Growth is only a good thing if you can trust the people around you to exceed your own expectations and take the pressure off you as an individual. There is little point in growing if you are clearing up after them and you don't feel like you can delegate.

Did you ever suffer from post-launch blues or a three-year itch?
Like any job you want to move on to doing the next best thing, inevitably there's a three-year itch! But as the master of your own destiny it is imperative that you keep your business ahead of the game – you should always be evolving.

How do you plan the 'next big thing'?
By making sure that the company is giving clients what they want, research what else you could offer and plan to add it on to your services.

If you could have known one thing when you started that you know now, what would it be?
That not everyone will be as committed as you are. Keep your shareholding lean and mean.

Is there anything else you'd like to pass on about growing or evolving your business?
Get the team around you right.

GORDON HAXTON, Owner, accountancy firm, 7 staff

What is the hardest thing about growing your business?
Developing a client base that will pay a market rate for your time.

Is growth always a good thing?
Not unless it is planned, controlled and cost effective. The desire for turnover is a false goal unless profit follows. The mantra is turnover is vanity, profit is sanity.

Did you ever suffer from post-launch blues or a three-year itch?
Not really.

How do you plan the 'next big thing'?
That's in the planning stage at the moment – new brand image, revised website, targeted marketing and so on.

If you could have known one thing when you started that you know now, what would it be?
To be more ambitious from day one. Have a medium-term plan and go for it, not deal in the short-term issues.

Is there anything else you'd like to pass on about growing or evolving your business?
It's not easy!

GREG MILLS, Owner, TV production company, 4 staff

What is the hardest thing about growing your business?
Committing to the inevitable increase in overhead.

Is growth always a good thing?
Literal answer – no. But it is always a good thing to consider it.

Did you ever suffer from post-launch blues or a three-year itch?
We started essentially out of adversity after having been let down by a previous business partner so it is fair to say that there

were some blues but it is nearly three years and no itch as things are currently getting better.

How do you plan the 'next big thing'?

Evolution seems to be working for us rather than concentrated planning.

If you could have known one thing when you started that you know now, what would it be?

Given the time in my life of starting the current business, I think it would be better if I had known less rather than more.

Is there anything else you'd like to pass on about growing or evolving your business?

Have fun with the people that you are in business with.

ROBERT RAY, Media agency director to sole trader, currently 10 staff

What is the hardest thing about growing your business?

Bureaucracy, cash flow and time.

Is growth always a good thing?

Hmm ... maybe, maybe not. Depends if it's at the expense of what your customers buy into and if it stretches your cash flow. For example, as a high-end consultant where people buy into 'you' then will they buy into someone else? What happens if you get a bad patch and they're on your payroll?

Did you ever suffer from post-launch blues or a three-year itch?

Yes – everyone must do I guess. But key is to remind yourself why you're doing it and look around. There are plenty of worse options! Seven-month itch is probably more realistic with most I know.

How do you plan the 'next big thing'?

Sudden inspirations rather than formal planning. Always have a pen and paper handy! Get good thinking time – a good run in the hills usually does it for me. And don't be too disheartened when you inevitably find that someone else has 'done' your idea already.

If you could have known one thing when you started that you know now, what would it be?

The total and all-consuming nature of your own thing. And all the needless paperwork!!!

Is there anything else you'd like to pass on about growing or evolving your business?

Don't be afraid to make mistakes. Just don't make the same mistake again and learn from the experience. Be willing to listen to customers and be quick to adapt your product or service – no one is loyal these days.

10–50 staff

JAMIE LISTER, Partner, marketing services company, 15 staff

What is the hardest thing about growing your business?

Getting the right people in at the right time to allow you to move on.

Is growth always a good thing?

Yes. There needs to be an end-game and if you're not growing then you are not moving towards achieving your objective.

Did you ever suffer from post-launch blues or a three-year itch?

Yes – got over them. Things might not be perfect, but they are a damned sight better than going through all the initial pain again.

How do you plan the 'next big thing'?

Work out what the next most important thing is for achieving the long-term plan and go and do it.

If you could have known one thing when you started that you know now, what would it be?

If you have a good plan, work hard and are smart enough, you will succeed.

Is there anything else you'd like to pass on about growing or evolving your business?

Stay focused – plan exactly what you want to be and treat other opportunities with suspicion.

MARK JOY, Partner, marketing agency, 21 staff

What is the hardest thing about growing your business?

The arbitrary nature of growth – often knowing where to put the effort in as so often the results come back where you least expect it. Having the commitment to prioritize properly and not simply try to do more of everything less well rather than identifying the right strategy and backing it.

Is growth always a good thing?

Not if it changes the thing about your business that most clients liked. Branding even for small business is crucial. If your first ten clients all picked you for being small and allowed you a good margin to give them a personal service, when they depart and you acquire your thirty-fifth client (who is no longer allowing you that margin), you may find yourself much worse off, closer to margin and unable to sell yourself as anything but 'medium'.

Did you ever suffer from post-launch blues or a three-year itch?

Yes – our third year saw our biggest client stop spending. We had grown every quarter for a year and a half before that and defined much of our business around that client. It led us not only to trade poorly for a while but also to conclude that businesses of our sort could only get 'so big' and that we might be wasting our time. If that hadn't happened we may have broken out from small-to-medium to medium by now, a key step.

How do you plan the 'next big thing'?

Make ourselves do the work. It is easy to be myopic and just get on with accounts hoping the next thing will just come along. You have to make time for planning, ask people for their input and make your plans. You then have to make sensible budget allocations and back your judgment.

If you could have known one thing when you started that you know now, what would it be?

The importance of doing new business work when the business is flourishing rather than waiting until you need it. The importance of your existing business in a growth strategy.

Is there anything else you'd like to pass on about growing or evolving your business?

Work out what you are good or great at and try to sell that hard rather than just trying to sell what you think the market wants today, as customers will see through you when you are selling things you aren't good at and you will have less business in the area in which you do excel.

RENÉE BOTHAM, Business growth specialists, 14 staff

What is the hardest thing about growing your business?

Finding the right people. Whether small or large, today no one in your organization is 'invisible' and you can't take risks for long. Our business is differentiated largely by the quality of our strategic input and intelligence and to take on someone who doesn't represent this is dangerous (tried once and burnt fingers). Also, ensuring that you are not just different to your competition, but ahead of the game. Working out what is going to be the next issue. We spend a lot on marketing intelligence, trends and information.

Is growth always a good thing?

Yes. No one thing ever remains the same. To stay as you are is impossible. Just as we as people need to 'grow', so does business.

Did you ever suffer from post-launch blues or a three-year itch?

No, never. I love this business even more now than I did when I set it up 17 years ago.

How do you plan the 'next big thing'?

Talking to bright people. Listening to what is happening around me both politically, and economically. Allowing myself the time away from day-to-day pressures to contemplate 'what else?'

If you could have known one thing when you started that you know now, what would it be?

One thing? Gosh, there's so much. Probably I'd have honed my financial skills. You need to see at a glance the comings and goings of your money.

Is there anything else you'd like to pass on about growing or evolving your business?

Believe in what you are doing and at the same time listen to healthy criticism. Surround yourself with people who are as passionate as you and have skills where you know you have weaknesses. Business is more than making money. It is in fact rather like a child growing up, so accept that there will be teething problems, and that it will face adolescent tantrums. It also needs to have an honest soul so treat all people as you would expect to be treated yourself. What you put in is largely what you get out. Take time out, because your business will be there when you get back and you will see more clearly what you are doing right as well as wrong, with the proper balance in your life.

AILSA WILLIAMS, Founder, media training company, 14 staff

What is the hardest thing about growing your business?

I guess it depends what your forte is. For me, staff management. Two, three, four staff no problem. Once we went from 10 to say 15, we found we needed much more formal processes to keep everyone on board and trying to achieve the same thing. Also it seems to be very easy to spend time managing staff rather than concentrating on the really important things.

Is growth always a good thing?

Always and at any cost, no. I guess it depends what you want to achieve. I think it is hard to stand still, so I would always go for growth, be it increasing turnover or maintaining turnover but increasing profitability.

Did you ever suffer from post-launch blues or a three-year itch?

No, seven-year itch, yes ... ten years definitely.

How do you plan the 'next big thing'?

Not sure.

If you could have known one thing when you started that you know now, what would it be?

EVERYTHING is negotiable.

Is there anything else you'd like to pass on about growing or evolving your business?

1 If you want it badly enough anything is possible.
2 Business is about making sales and cash flow. If you keep an eye on those two, everything else can be managed.
3 Prioritize – do the important things first, don't put them off.
4 Client service – most businesses (in the UK) are so bad at it that being better than the competition is easy to do and gives you a huge advantage.

ALEX AIKEN, Head of communications, city council, 22 staff

What is the hardest thing about growing your business?

After winning the first few contracts, finding the right people to expand the work.

Is growth always a good thing?

No, it can dilute the quality of the offer to existing clients, which can in turn destroy the business.

Did you ever suffer from post-launch blues or a three-year itch?
Yes.

How do you plan the 'next big thing'?
By thinking through where we need to be and then working out the three steps that will get us there.

If you could have known one thing when you started that you know now, what would it be?
The real costs of doing business – all the hidden extras around employing people.

MARTIN ROBERTS, Partner, integrated marketing agency, 20 staff

What is the hardest thing about growing your business?
Being in the right shape to capitalize on opportunities.

Is growth always a good thing?
Yes – standing still is certain death.

Did you ever suffer from post-launch blues or a three-year itch?
No – always hungry!

How do you plan the 'next big thing'?
Based entirely on market trends, research, studious scrutiny of the competition and educated guess work.

If you could have known one thing when you started that you know now, what would it be?
Work on your business not in it. The three ways to grow your business (more punters, increased frequency and increased value of sale).

Is there anything else you'd like to pass on about growing or evolving your business?
Be absolutely committed to what you do – this is MUCH more than just being interested. Successful businesses are the ones that add greater value than their competitors. Strive to build the strongest possible rapport between you and your customers. Know the difference between a sale and a customer. Never, ever forget the importance of after sales. Never, ever ignore your competition. Never, ever think you're safe. Absolutely every cliché about cash being king is right. Do EVERYTHING you can to let cash flow into your business. Take no prisoners with credit control! You CAN be too busy!

GARY MILLER-CHEEVERS, Founder, financial loans business, 20 staff

What is the hardest thing about growing your business?
Saving today's income for tomorrow's expansion.

Is growth always a good thing?
No.

Did you ever suffer from post-launch blues or a three-year itch?
Never heard of it.

How do you plan the 'next big thing'?
Business is about evolution.

If you could have known one thing when you started that you know now, what would it be?
Don't waste money on marketing.

Is there anything else you'd like to pass on about growing or evolving your business?
Don't waste money on anything.

LAUREN RICHARDS, Founder, public relations agency, 14 staff

What is the hardest thing about growing your business?
The main challenge is finding the right staff. It is important that an SME business retains its 'can do' culture and therefore hiring the right team is vitally important as otherwise it is impossible to grow because the management becomes a bottleneck.

Is growth always a good thing?
If growth is too rapid it will negatively impact the business as quality suffers. However, it is impossible to stand still. You are either growing or shrinking so steady growth is always a good thing.

Did you ever suffer from post-launch blues or a three-year itch?
It can be difficult to motivate yourself if you find that you are facing the same problems over and over again so it is important to get external help such as a good non-exec director who can offer a different perspective and a less emotional response. This can help you to solve the problems that make you feel like you are going round in circles.

If you could have known one thing when you started that you know now, what would it be?

I think it is that once you run your own business you will never switch off. You will be constantly thinking about it. This doesn't matter as long as you are enjoying your job but it is a mistake to start a business thinking it will give you a better work–life balance than working for someone else. You can sometimes spend less time in the office but you will spend a lot more time thinking about work.

GILES GIBBONS, Founder, social marketing consultancy, 15 staff

What is the hardest thing about growing your business?

Risking what you have built up so far.

Is growth always a good thing?

No.

Did you ever suffer from post-launch blues or a three-year itch?

Multiple itches (normally when things are slow).

How do you plan the 'next big thing'?

Not strategically enough.

If you could have known one thing when you started that you know now, what would it be?

You have to invest to reap returns (not just hard work).

Is there anything else you'd like to pass on about growing or evolving your business?

Build a company that is right for you, not what you think companies are meant to be like. If you only want to work two days a week, then build a company around that.

TOM HOLMES, Founder, creative services company, 15 staff

What is the hardest thing about growing your business?

Identifying the right person or people that will help you make it happen.

Is growth always a good thing?

Yes, if the integrity of your product or service doesn't suffer.

Did you ever suffer from post-launch blues or a three-year itch?

No, just the loneliness of the long distance runner.

How do you plan the 'next big thing'?
I don't. My business is the next big thing.

If you could have known one thing when you started that you know now, what would it be?
It takes a lot longer than you think.

Is there anything else you'd like to pass on about growing or evolving your business?
Listen to your clients, keep your business proposition simple and hire hungry, enthusiastic people to deliver it and reward them when they do.

NEIL DUFFY, Managing director, advertising agency, 40 staff

What is the hardest thing about growing your business?
Choosing the correct strategic direction to take and being able to implement it. Your business needs to have a clear understanding of why it exists and what it is good at. If this is understood and believed in internally, it becomes much easier to communicate externally and more attractive to potential new clients.

Is growth always a good thing?
Not always but mostly. Growth has to be in line with the strategic aims of the organization. If not, then those aims are diluted. Equally, growth should be a consequence of doing what you do well, rather than a central aim of the company in itself. In the latter instance, there is a strong risk of alienating your current client base by over concentration on new client acquisition. However, if managed properly, growth provides the ability to enhance the service that you offer to your current client base, as well as develop your people and give a greater breadth to your scope for managing the development of the business.

Did you ever suffer from post-launch blues or a three-year itch?
All the time. But that's not a bad thing. You should continually question what your company does and how well it does it. It can be frustrating and uncomfortable if that is difficult to maintain or to communicate, but it is better than risking complacency.

How do you plan the 'next big thing'?
This depends on what 'the next big thing' is. All innovation should be grounded in the skills base of your company. You

should constantly review to ensure that you are doing what you should do properly and see where improvement can be made. That may result in being able to identify an area where you can truly innovate and which will be of interest to your current clients and potential new clients. If the 'next big thing' is thought up and developed in isolation, it is likely that it won't be that big a thing in the long term.

If you could have known one thing when you started that you know now, what would it be?

You have much more space to be radical in how you run your company than you think. There is a tendency to try to fit your service and offer around the people and the assets that you have, rather than examine how best to do what you are best at.

Is there anything else that you would like to pass on about growing or evolving your business?

Talk things through with friends, peers, colleagues and even rivals. It is amazing how many people have a genuine and unselfish interest in your business and also what interesting pieces of insight and advice that they are prepared to share.

BELINDA LAWSON, Owner, public relations agency, 15 staff

What is the hardest thing about growing your business?
Finding the time to dream, review, plan and then stick with it.

Is growth always a good thing?
Yes – without growth there is no ambition, and without ambition I believe you slide backwards.

Did you ever suffer from post-launch blues or a three-year itch?
Yes, it can be very frustrating especially if you've come from a larger company to be small and treated as small.

How do you plan the 'next big thing'?
I am not sure that there is always that much planning. There is always a vision or dream and from somewhere an idea comes that feels spot on.

If you could have known one thing when you started that you know now, what would it be?
Be braver and trust your instincts.

Is there anything else you'd like to pass on about growing or evolving your business?

Never be afraid to ask advice from someone you admire.

MARTIN DEBOO, Partner, communications strategy company, 30 staff

What is the hardest thing about growing your business?

I'm not an entrepreneur as you know and therefore find it difficult to comment on a lot of the specifics. However, one overall belief that I have about growth is that 'you don't have to win by much to win by a lot'. The issue is that of the virtues of compound growth. Consider two scenarios:

1 If you can grow a business by 5 per cent for ten years rather than 2 per cent (i.e. two-and-a-half times as fast) you will end up with three times the additional sales ... and probably more than three times the incremental profit and much enhanced exit multiple
2 Steady growth at, say, 5 per cent for ten years is better than four years growth at 15 per cent per annum, then stasis or decline.

Maybe a rather conservative message for your intended audience of hot honchos but it has struck me recently how, for companies like Tesco and P&G, quite small differences in sales growth and margin translate into big differences in shareholder value.

PAUL SPEERS, Owner, IT services company, 20 staff

What is the hardest thing about growing your business?

Getting the right staff for the right money.

Is growth always a good thing?

No, profit is. If the two are managed well, then yes.

How do you plan the 'next big thing'?

It finds you if you are doing the right things.

If you could have known one thing when you started that you know now, what would it be?

Business is not personal. It's business, so treat it that way! Bitterness is not in the dictionary of the entrepreneur. If it is, then see section entitled: 'Waste of time: being bitter.'

Is there anything else you'd like to pass on about growing or evolving your business?
Watch the figures like a hawk and believe them. Seek guidance from an independent business consultant or Managing Director.

GILES FRASER, Co-founder, public relations agency, 40 staff

What is the hardest thing about growing your business?
Balancing the need for structure, process and systems with the requirement to keep the fleet-footedness of the start-up.

Is growth always a good thing?
Depends on the type of business. In a service business you should only grow as fast as your ability to pass on the culture and way of doing things to new people. Grow too fast and you dilute what enabled you to grow in the first place.

Did you ever suffer from post-launch blues or a three-year itch?
No.

How do you plan the 'next big thing'?
Listen to our clients, look how successful businesses managed expansion strategies in other sectors and test it out with lots of people you know before you make a decision.

If you could have known one thing when you started that you know now, what would it be?
If you think you have reached the right decision don't hesitate. Your first instincts are normally right.

Is there anything else you'd like to pass on about growing or evolving your business?
Just because you have been successful in the past doesn't mean you are going to be successful in the future. Never be complacent, always seek to improve, innovate and re-invent your offer.

PAUL EPHREMSEN, Founder, brand experience agency, 42 staff

What is the hardest thing about growing your business?
Different skills required to set up a business as opposed to grow a business. Entrepreneurs have skills to set up, but this doesn't mean they have those for growth such as leadership, strategy, systems and controls, finance skills. The difficult bit is identifying talent to bring these skills in – if we don't have the

skills how can we effectively select people who do?! For example, interviewing finance directors is extremely difficult!

Is growth always a good thing?
Depends on your lifestyle objectives. If you want a comfortable living and low stress then growth is probably not top of the agenda. Growth is good if it brings stability and certainty to a business. Thereafter the desire for growth from a wealth, ego or power perspective must be weighed up against the negatives in terms of stress, skills to achieve, and overall complexity of life it brings with it.

Did you ever suffer from post-launch blues or a three-year itch?
No! I do need the business to invent challenges for itself periodically – re-branding, relaunching services etc., which keeps the stimulation going.

How do you plan the 'next big thing'?
Normally very random – on the running machine or in the shower! Very rarely do we sit in a meeting to discuss our next plans formally.

If you could have known one thing when you started that you know now, what would it be?
That the audience we are selling to know less about our subject matter than we do. We always felt like the new boys and our confidence suffered as a consequence. If we had known this from the start our growth would have been quicker.

Is there anything else you'd like to pass on about growing or evolving your business?
My golden rules if I did it again:

- Select the right business advisers from the start – don't just phone the first you see in *Yellow Pages*!
- Tie key staff in with incentives and be generous, but identify those that are key and those that are not.
- Be absolutely clear about what your product or service is and focus, focus, focus – this will ensure your clients (and your internal team) have a total understanding about the business's reason for being.
- Create a distinct business culture – it will reward you in the long run with loyal, motivated staff.
- Decide how you are going to maintain the same service levels as you grow and you are relying on others to deliver them.

- Make sure your financial reporting systems and team are strong before you deliver an aggressive growth plan.
- Cash and funding are critical – be pessimistic.
- Keep a close eye on overheads in the early years.

CHRIS MATTHEWS, Founder, public relations agency, 25 staff

What is the hardest thing about growing your business?

If you have been used to running a large and well-known company previously, then it's recognizing that a new set of rules apply to growing a smaller firm. It's harder as, to begin with, the name recognition isn't there and you have to be twice as good as the opposition to be perceived as doing as good a job.

Is growth always a good thing?

No, not if it takes you away from being the type of business you intend to be. You have to turn away the 'wrong' sort of opportunities and that's not always easy.

Did you ever suffer from post-launch blues or a three-year itch?

No – what does happen is that you come to the end of a honeymoon period and you can lose clients or staff. The secret is to tell yourself in advance that it's going to happen, so you are prepared for the emotional shock when it arrives.

How do you plan the 'next big thing'?

You have to continue to reinvent your business all the time, as business models become out of date (even if only at the edges) in a frighteningly short space of time. It's the constant planning and executing; planning and executing that enable you to face fresh challenges. If you wait and deal with the next big thing as a solus event, it becomes a much bigger challenge. It's the same trap as companies having an annual strategy event – strategy is something you should look at regularly, not once a year in an awayday.

If you could have known one thing when you started that you know now, what would it be?

Get the business plan or structure right, at the outset. Once you have started, it's too late to go back and change things. So plan, plan, plan; test, test, test, before you set up.

Afterthought

I've been giving this more thought. I'm pleased to say our company is doing well at the moment. I think we are doing better than our peers who started up in business at about the same time as us. Thinking about why we are flourishing and they seem not to be, it struck me that we appointed a non-executive Chairman at the outset (he was very much part of our planning since inception, actually). He has proved to be a potent 'secret weapon', as his experience is invaluable and he has the ability to defuse matters which, if left unchecked, could escalate to threaten relationships amongst the other shareholders. Anyone setting up in business should give serious thought to acquiring such a Chairman.

IAN FAIRBROTHER, Founder, media auditing business, 33 staff

What is the hardest thing about growing your business?
Finding and keeping the right people.

Is growth always a good thing?
No.

Did you ever suffer from post-launch blues or a three-year itch?
No. I was advised to give it at least 18 months – after about six I knew I would never want to work for anyone else again.

How do you plan the 'next big thing'?
You don't, it plans you.

If you could have known one thing when you started that you know now, what would it be?
Getting established in a proper office of your own does wonders for the confidence.

Is there anything else you'd like to pass on about growing or evolving your business?
Get a good lawyer and accountant and don't believe that banks are there to help.

More than 50 staff

PHIL GEORGIADIS, Partner, media agency, 50 staff

What is the hardest thing about growing your business?
Building the right team.

Is growth always a good thing?
Yes.

Did you ever suffer from post-launch blues or a three-year itch?
Yes ... lasted for five years!

How do you plan the 'next big thing'?
With difficulty as we are risk averse and doing all right without it.

If you could have known one thing when you started that you know now, what would it be?
Good things come to those who wait and most new business is never more than a learning curve.

Is there anything else you'd like to pass on about growing or evolving your business?
Don't hesitate to give it a go as long as you have a clear sense of purpose and at least one partner.

STUART ROCK, Owner, Publishing Company, 65 staff

What is the hardest thing about growing your business?
Having the right people in the right place at the appropriate time in the growth/size of the business. Someone who is fantastic at the start can be out of their depth later on – and not recognize the fact.

Is growth always a good thing?
Yes. No growth means no attraction or retention of good people. Decide from the outset whether you want to grow the business – and on what scale.

Did you ever suffer from post-launch blues or a three-year itch?
No. That's a good thing about growing a business. There's always something new.

How do you plan the 'next big thing'?
Conversation. Chitchat. Drinks with experts. Fans of your first product telling you what you should do next. Read lots – and read laterally.

If you could have known one thing when you started that you know now, what would it be?
Few other people are as excited by your business as you are.

Is there anything else you'd like to pass on about growing or evolving your business?
Be serious from the outset about your customer data, what you know about them, and also about your own internal knowledge. It might be boring at the start but just wait until you

have hundreds or thousands of customers and you realize that you haven't got the systems in place to tell you anything meaningful about them. Marketing meets technology meets knowledge management ... that's the basis of a great business in the future.

SHAUN ORPEN, Telecoms marketing director, 50 staff

What is the hardest thing about growing your business?

It is making that first step – have you got enough new business to take on extra resource. Do you indeed want to develop a growing business? I believe you need to be clear about whether you want to grow or not. As a small business, you may also have the added challenge of needing time to do the sales and marketing for more capacity, when in reality it is hard enough to create the time to create the current level of demand.

Is growth always a good thing?

Instead of saying whether growth is always good or bad – there can be times when both apply. I do, however, believe in today's world it is dangerous to stand still. Competition is always on your heels. Generally I do believe that growth is a good thing, however it is important not to compromise your strategic goals and try to move out of a niche, without it being a conscious decision.

How do you plan the 'next big thing'?

With energy, passion and insight! It can be very hard – creating specific stimulus can help. For example, running customer workshops, external market reports, reading about some new technology.

If you could have known one thing when you started that you know now, what would it be?

In the development stage of the business, instead of trying to get the proposition perfect before selling it, use an iterative development process to build some early customers.

LOUISE WALL, Recruitment consultant, 52 staff

What is the hardest thing about growing your business?

Managing the transition in terms of people, process and profit. Maintaining standards and culture. Keeping ahead of the game in terms of investment and strategic change. Avoiding going after everything that moves. Having a clear proposition.

Is growth always a good thing?

No, not always. Sometimes small, swift and smart is beautiful and it helps stick to the knitting rather than getting lost in offering too many services that are neither profitable nor rewarding in the product sense.

Did you ever suffer from post-launch blues or a three-year itch?

Yes, naturally. How do you keep the momentum and the freshness? Partners will also experience this, so you need to be aware and act sensitively and professionally.

How do you plan the 'next big thing'?

It is better to take a calculated risk than a risk without knowing the consequences.

If you could have known one thing when you started that you know now, what would it be?

Know who to trust, work with complimentary talent, and always act and tell the truth fast.

Is there anything else you would like to pass on about growing or evolving your business?

Be smart, do the proper due diligence, listen to the market. Do not over invest, be clear and focused in your proposition. Work with clients and people you like and respect.

LAURENCE GREEN, Partner, Advertising agency, 90 staff

What is the hardest thing about growing your business?

In advertising, that too much growth is predicated on pitching for business. The willing diversion of your best people – for free, for several weeks at a time – from your paying clients and best (organic growth) prospects.

Is growth always a good thing?

If you're trying to build a business for the short-term, (i.e. a quick exit), then yes. If you're trying to build a brand and/or culture of more permanence, then you can grow too fast. The wrong clients, the wrong results can set you back a long way in a people business.

Did you ever suffer from post-launch blues or a three-year itch?

Not really. But at three years you realize the business will never be 'finished', that new challenges emerge to fit the time available!

How do you plan the 'next big thing'?
With difficulty. The day job gets in the way!

If you could have known one thing when you started that you know now, what would it be?
That a business comprising five equal partners can be a curse as well as a blessing. That clear roles – if not hierarchies – must be established.

CLAIRE WALKER, Founder, public relations agency, 65 staff

What is the hardest thing about growing your business?
Remembering that you have a family and a private life and being a workaholic is boring for the people who might meet you whether through work or outside of work. If you're not an 'interesting person' people won't want to do business with you. Keep true to you, 'the person', don't become 'the business'.

Is growth always a good thing?
No, profit is a good thing. Growth doesn't necessarily matter. You can reward people and also develop new areas of the business if you are profitable. Growth is good and it offers people career paths etc., but it's a complete fallacy that money isn't everything. Money talks and people want to be financially rewarded well.

Did you ever suffer from post-launch blues or a three-year itch?
After a few months I wondered if I would ever get my life back, or be able to go on holiday. Every now and then I dream of jacking it all in to be a lumberjack or something completely physical, and with no responsibility for anyone or anything. It passes through, and 98 times out of 100 I'm more than delighted with running my own business. The only thing that has eclipsed it is having a baby. In fact, launching a business is a bit like having a baby And you get the sleepless nights and metaphorical dirty nappies to deal with in the first two years too.

How do you plan the 'next big thing'?
I'm never short of the next big thing – choosing which one is difficult. Priority is key or you can stretch like an elastic band. My ambitions for the company are always way beyond our current reach but that spurs me on. I have these thoughts when I'm away from the business, never when I'm sitting at my desk. You need to get away from the business to have the enlightening moments of inspiration.

If you could have known one thing when you started that you know now, what would it be?

That you can't be good at everything and if you can't add up and you're a bit short on organisational skills and process, get a person who is to do your finances and chase in the money. Likewise if you like writing the invoices and counting the money, get someone in who can sell like hell. Play to your personal strengths and surround yourself with people who more than make up for your weaknesses.

Is there anything else you'd like to pass on about growing or evolving your business?

Never talk about it as 'your' business. Everyone who works for you or who has worked for you has had a role in the success of your business. Recognize and reward them for that – verbally if not financially. The person who thinks they did it all by themselves will be either a very lonely person or will have a revolving door of people coming and going. Let everyone feel it's their business and let everyone have a clear role in the development and progression of the business – but never let more than 50 per cent of the shares go if you want to stay in control.

PAUL SIMONS, Multiple CEO roles, business owner

What is the hardest thing about growing your business?

In a service business the servicing of current clients takes total precedence. Therefore dedicating resource to future business is often put on the backburner. The result is many businesses hit a glass ceiling of revenue and can't break through to the next level. It is very difficult to take the hard decision and divide the senior team into today and tomorrow.

Is growth always a good thing?

Yes, definitely. All businesses are a leaky bucket, income draining out of the hole in the bottom. There has to be a mentality of growth otherwise every business will stall. A good discipline is to assume 10 per cent minimum of income will evaporate in the next year, but target 20 per cent growth giving a new business target of 30 per cent incremental income. This sharpens the mind and will probably deliver 15 per cent growth.

Did you ever suffer from post-launch blues or a three-year itch?

Yes, everyone does. The excitement of the first year or so is replaced by constant anxieties about the business and inevitably earning less money than your mates working for a big company. The payday seems a very long way off.

How do you plan the 'next big thing'?

It is essential to have an annual day of reflection – the past, present and future. Doing more of the same is death. Each year have one new initiative, be prepared to try and fail because one will succeed. Keep the business fresh, maintain excitement, and back the people who have ideas.

If you could have known one thing when you started that you know now, what would it be?

Whilst we did have excellent financial management, the one thing that I underestimated was the critical importance of matching growth with cash flow management. Cash is king, profit is clearly essential but when the profit is generated, it may not match the needs of the business in terms of surplus cash. I found the banks utterly useless in supporting a rapidly growing business. They were inflexible, they always turned a drama into a crisis, and they seemed to get more anxious the more successful the business became. So my mantra would be: cash is king, never be caught short.

Is there anything else you'd like to pass on about growing or evolving your business?

My advice to anyone considering their business future would be to have Big Audacious Goals. A 10 per cent growth in income each year is fine but not exactly exciting. I have been fortunate to work with people who have crazy goals and it's funny how they seem to do very well compared with the people who plod along. Apologies to Leo Burnett because I'll get this wrong but he said something like 'If you reach for the stars you might not quite get there but you won't come up with a handful of mud either'. Too right.

VANELLA JACKSON, Managing director, research agency, 70 staff

What is the hardest thing about growing your business?

Managing the demands of new business, whilst keeping existing clients happy.

Is growth always a good thing?

Not always ... but it keeps morale high and new opportunities and challenges to keep us fresh and on our toes.

Did you ever suffer from post-launch blues or a three-year itch?

Yes, don't we all? We wouldn't be human otherwise.

How do you plan the 'next big thing'?
Spend some time thinking about it.

If you could have known one thing when you started that you know now, what would it be?
It is always about people, people, people.

Is there anything else you'd like to pass on about growing or evolving your business?
Keep clients happy. They are your best new business tool (more work from them, more work from them telling others how great you are).

NICK MUSTOE, Owner, advertising agency, 70 staff

What is the hardest thing about growing your business?
Finding people with the necessary passion and talent to ensure the culture and style of the agency doesn't get diluted.

Is growth always a good thing?
No! Momentum is important but size in and of itself is frequently a two-edged sword.

Did you ever suffer from post-launch blues or a three-year itch?
No! But I didn't appreciate the huge difference in commitment between a senior position in someone else's company against having your own company.

How do you plan the 'next big thing'?
Always start with the people, the casting.

If you could have known one thing when you started that you know now, what would it be?
Talented craftsmen are by no means talented managers.

Is there anything else you'd like to pass on about growing or evolving your business?
You have to enjoy it!!

JONATHAN HARMAN, CEO, communications agency, 60 staff

What's the hardest part about growing your business?
Finding the time to invest in growth because this time earns me money tomorrow yet my staff and shareholders need to be paid today.

Is growth always a good thing?

Only if you are prepared to accept the structural implications, including for your own role. The larger the company becomes, the more you have to let others do for you. This is not always easy for a control freak. It is also not good if you are growing in areas you are not expert in. You'll be found out eventually and it'll cost you dearly in time, money and, worst of all, reputation.

Do you ever suffer from post launch blues or three-year itch?

No. The day you decide there is nothing more you can do to improve your business you should do two things. Firstly, fire anyone who agrees with you and then resign yourself. No three-year itch, but it is stressful working with idiots.

How do you plan the 'next big thing'?

Be constantly dissatisfied with the status quo. Imagine a place you would love to be in a few years time that is only just realistic, then plot a route there in three-month increments.

If you could have known one thing when you started that you know now, what would it be?

Business is fundamentally simple: revenue minus costs equals profit.

Anything else you would like to pass on about growing a business?

Beware of the cost of sale – the up-front investment has to be commensurate with the reward for success.

TONY WALFORD, Financial and commercial director, branding agency, 100 staff

What is the hardest thing about growing your business?

Quality organic revenue growth. It is my view that we should not acquire businesses in the same market as ourselves to increase our client list. We should have good enough people to win the pitches and grow it organically as it is. You should only acquire businesses to add skill sets you do not already have. Getting the quality people who can develop and add new accounts is the hardest thing.

Is growth always a good thing?

Only if it is profitable. Many businesses view growth as being measured in terms of increase in revenue. This is particularly true in service sector businesses, which tend to have league tables based on turnover. There is no point in taking on projects if it is not cost effective to work them. You can see plenty of businesses that show a percentage increase in revenue outstripping the increase in profitability (in some cases, turnover goes up, profit goes down). I have two recent examples where we have actually walked away from the final stage of a pitch because what we were being asked to do for the money just did not make sense. Revenue is vanity, profit is sanity.

Did you ever suffer from post-launch blues or a three-year itch?
Yes. Part of being an entrepreneur is that you don't want to 'drive the car' long term after you have built it! It is better to have the idea, build the car, then employ someone else to drive it for you whilst you go build the next one.

How do you plan the 'next big thing'?
In terms of new ideas, they just happen through moments of inspiration or opportunistically. I find that if I sit and try and come up with an idea, it doesn't happen. In terms of moving into novel related areas within a business, external consultants/facilitators can help. This is because often it is difficult to see what can be done when you are deep into a business and having a facilitator can focus brainstorming.

If you could have known one thing when you started that you know now, what would it be?
Not to keep pursuing something that you have built if it isn't a success. Some things you do work, some don't. If you have a dead horse on your hands, don't waste time flogging it forever. Set yourself a limit as to how much time you will put in to your 'Problem Child' and, once that limit is reached, drop it and move on to the next thing.

Is there anything else you'd like to pass on about growing or evolving your business?
Keep the management team small and only have people on the board/in the management team who are good at managing. There is a temptation to reward by giving directorships to people who have performed really well in the tasks they do, but they may not necessarily have the qualities to manage a business. Additionally, they may not actually want to take on, or be aware of, the fiduciary responsibilities that come with being a director. Business evolution over the years has dictated this myth that to be a success you ultimately become a director. This is, however, wrong. Reward people for excellent performance and make them champions in their own right, but only have a management team consisting of those that can manage.

CHRIS HIRST, Managing director, advertising agency, 216 staff

What is the hardest thing about growing your business?

Balancing the often-conflicting objectives the new business pitch process throws up. Under usual circumstances we very much believe in making the right recommendation to solve the client's business or communications problem. In a pitch the objective is to win the pitch. These two are not the same thing.

Is growth always a good thing?

By and large yes. I think it is certainly better than the opposite. It is possible to think of examples where agencies appear to have grown too fast or grown in a way which conflicts with their founding ethos, but I think this is about the quality of the management rather than the volume of business.

Did you ever suffer from post-launch blues or a three-year itch?

I have never run a start-up, but my observation is that it often happens. This is usually about managing size, direction, the development of the partners as leaders and managers, and so on. I observe that many advertising agencies get to a size of around 70–80 and hit a real inflection point: will they power on through and become an enduring brand, or will they stutter, or, worse, retract?

Personally I think this is a function of:

- i Size: suddenly you can't do everything yourself (as a founder).
- ii Leadership: you have to begin to lead and inspire others – it's not enough to be small, new and groovy.
- iii Vision: you have to decide what you are about, what your personal and business objectives are (and more importantly get your partners to agree).
- iv You're not the new kid on the block any more – so you have to work harder to get your message across (to new clients, existing clients, the media, employees, etc.).
- v Reality bites: you have to start to spend time worrying about grown-up issues like staff retention, office management, human resources, a bigger building, your founding client getting their own three-year itch, and so on.

How do you plan the 'next big thing'?

Difficult. I think there are two main styles:

- i Scattergun: some people are just very lateral and very inventive – some of their ideas are inspired, some inevitably not. In this circumstance the business almost becomes an 'energy brand', feeding on the leaders' exciting proposals, and accepting that some will thrive and others not.

At the other end of the spectrum:

ii Institutionalized: the leadership team has to accept and understand that this is an important priority and work (as a team) and in the context of the agreed business vision and objectives towards the generation and execution of 'The Next Big Thing'. I guess this is about blood sweat, tears and (crucially) making it a priority.

I don't know which I prefer.

If you could have known one thing when you started that you know now, what would it be?
The job never feels done (because it never is).

KIRSTEN ENGLISH, Telecoms general manager, 400 staff

What is the hardest thing about growing your business?
Getting real scale.

Is growth always a good thing?
Not unless it has margin associated with it and is synergistic with whatever the current core business is. In the early start of a company there are often not all the systems and processes in place and this leads to more hands on. There is probably a model of higher costs, pruning costs followed by growth again.

Did you ever suffer from post-launch blues or a three-year itch?
Post-launch blues yes. Three-year itch yes.

How do you plan the 'next big thing'?
Look at what you have and see every permutation to iterate it. Look at the competition. Examine market trends. Then when you are fully appraised read all the papers you can to get ideas, speak with the market and customers. Then think very hard for something innovative – stealing from other industries where appropriate.

If you could have known one thing when you started that you know now, what would it be?
There really is more money and opportunity in America – but not always the attitude or brainpower to make it work – lots of mediocrity. Would perhaps have moved over there for my business in light of this knowledge.

Is there anything else you'd like to pass on about growing or evolving your business?
You need a very good management team to succeed.

RICHARD HYTNER, Chairman, advertising agency, 500 staff

What is the hardest thing about growing your business?
The tyranny of being busy, attending to the urgent and unimportant.

Is growth always a good thing?
Not if it's out of whack with your company's purpose and what you are passionate about.

Did you ever suffer from post-launch blues or a three-year itch?
If only I could stretch the itch to three years. Restlessness kicks in for me every 18 months.

How do you plan the 'next big thing'?
Way before I am unhappy with 'the existing big thing'.

If you could have known one thing when you started that you know now, what would it be?
Something I learnt from my boss: Attend first thing to the issue that's weighing on your mind most. The rest of the day will be a joy. It works.

Is there anything else you'd like to pass on about growing or evolving your business?
Be yourself.

JIM MARSHALL, Chairman, media agency, 280 staff

What is the hardest thing about growing your business?
Getting started! Growth of course is both the dream and the objective of any business – through controlled and profitable growth. The most effective and quickest way to achieve growth is through reputation, profile and success. And the most effective way of achieving these is through growth! The vicious circle. So there has to be a strategy to 'kick-start' the growth of the business. Managed growth is important, but the problem of managing growth is a good problem to have, managing a lack of growth is a bad problem to have.

Is growth always a good thing?
I would say generally yes, even if it does prove testing from time to time. The only time it becomes negative is if or when it

undermines your ability to service existing clients. Culturally, this is a very bad strategy – we all know that poor reputations are built on treating existing or established customers cynically.

Commercially, it's extremely hazardous. It could, and often does, result in fractured relationships with longer term customers and lost business. This in turn can start to undermine the reputation and stability of the overall business.

Did you ever suffer from post-launch blues or a three-year itch?

I wouldn't say post-launch blues, or even a three-year itch. However, I think you have to recognize that there are going to be times when your business will be in fashion and those when it won't. The trick, in my view at least, is never to believe your own propaganda, i.e. 'When you're being told you're great, you won't be that great, and when you're told you're rubbish, you won't be that rubbish.'

How do you plan the 'next big thing'?

In my experience the 'big thing' is actually never quite that big (unless of course you are a porn star and are prepared to have the surgery). Big things in business become big, because you recognize a market development and then invest in developing expertise in that area. But it always takes longer than you hope or expect and therefore you should always plan for the longer term. The longer term is more rewarding anyway – both commercially and culturally.

If you could have known one thing when you started that you know now, what would it be?

Forget customer relationships, contacts generally, recent experience etc. Your only real and most valuable asset is your talent. If you undervalue it, don't expect anyone else to put a higher value on it.

Is there anything else you'd like to pass on about growing or evolving your business?

Enjoy it, if you don't, don't do it. In fact if you have any reservations, don't do it. (Businesses, when you own or part-own them, are more difficult and even more costly than marriages to extract yourself from. So beware of the commitment!)

Teach Yourself Running your own Business, Kevin Duncan (Hodder & Stoughton, 2005)

The Tipping Point, Malcolm Gladwell (Little, Brown, 2000)

Blink, Malcom Gladwell (Little, Brown, 2005)

Flicking your Creative Switch, Wayne Lotherington (John Wiley & Sons, 2003)

The Economist Guide to Management Ideas, Tim Hindle (Profile, 2003)

Eating the Big Fish, Adam Morgan (John Wiley & Sons, 1999)

The Pirate Inside, Adam Morgan (John Wiley & Sons, 2004)

Simply Brilliant, Fergus O'Connell (Pearson, 2004)

Six Thinking Hats, Edward de Bono (Penguin, 1999)

The Entrepreneur's Book of Checklists, Robert Ashton (Pearson, 2004)

index

teach yourself

business plans

polly bird

- Do you need to prepare a business plan?
- Are you worried about what to include and what to exclude?

If you are preparing a business plan, whether for short-term financial backing or for long-term planning, you will need guidance on what to present, and how to present it. **Business Plans** will help you define your business, know your market and explain the finances of your company. By tackling the task of writing a business plan head on, this book will help you to prepare and present your plan with confidence.

Polly Bird is a professional writer of business and training books.

teach yourself

setting up a small business

vera hughes & david weller

- Are you setting up a small business?
- Do you need help to define your product or service?
- Are you looking for guidance in marketing and finance?

Setting Up a Small Business helps you with all the everyday aspects of running a small business and gives detailed guidance on specialized areas such as legal requirements, opening a retail or office-based business, staff selection and marketing.

Vera Hughes and **David Weller** started their own business in 1980, having been involved in the retail industry for many years. They have written a number of books on retailing.

teach yourself

marketing

j. jonathan gabay

- Do you want to understand the principles of marketing?
- Do you need to promote your business, product or organization more effectively?
- Are you looking for more creative marketing ideas?

Marketing concentrates on the engine which drives successful marketing – imagination. Revealing many profitable tips and secrets to help you target, brand and sell your enterprise whilst generating provocative publicity, this book will keep you three steps ahead of the competition.

J. Jonathan Gabay is an award-winning copywriter, course director at the Chartered Institute of Marketing, the world's biggest marketing training organization, and director of a creative marketing consultancy firm.

teach yourself

PR

angela murray

- Do you want to design and implement a PR campaign?
- Are you planning to work with external PR consultants?
- Do you need to gain media coverage for your business?

PR is a practical, no-nonsense guide to implementing realistic and successful PR campaigns. It covers all aspects of the field, including media liaison, using PR professionals, crisis management, internal PR, careers in PR and current trends and technologies, and will help you to distinguish your business from the competition.

Angela Murray is a freelance PR consultant who has advised a wide range of businesses, from multinationals to small organizations.